Haunted Texas Highways

Legends & Lore of the Lone Star State

Edited by
Joy Nord

ISBN
1-933177-39-X (10 digit)
978-1-933177-39-7 (13 digit)

Library of Congress Control Number: 2012943854

First Edition

Printed in the United States of America
Published by Atriad Press LLC
2112 Homestead Dr.
Mesquite, TX 75181
www.atriadpress.com

Table of Contents

Acknowledgments

Although my name may appear on the cover of this book, there are numerous people who have contributed to its creation. To compile an anthology requires the input from many people. I want to thank everyone who contributed: the storytellers, the writers, the researchers, and the critique partners. Special thanks must also be given to those people who shared their ghostly encounters and allowed the author to use their name and location, to which you will be introduced in the following stories.

Some stories required intense research. With only so much information available, the authors did a remarkable job. There are unsubstantiated stories in all fifty states that tell of haunted highways, but many of the highways, roads, or bridges never existed and were just the figments of the storyteller's imagination; however, this book about Texas is well supported. Some stories in this book are considered only to be legend, but they were too well known to be left out. Each story is special and has its own unique voice.

Thanks to everyone at Atriad Press for the support and patience with me while I gathered the stories for this book.

And last but not least, I must thank my husband, Richard Nord, who has driven me all over Texas as I searched for stories, attended workshops and/or conferences so that I could learn the writing craft and publishing business. He also spent countless hours at my computer, correcting my errors. Without his help there would not be a book.

Introduction

Texas, a land of legends and folklore, can out-tell any other state when it comes to whipping out a good ghost story—whether fact or fiction.

If you're ready to take a haunted road trip without leaving the comfort of your favorite recliner, then this book is for you. The journey stretches across Texas from west to east. Just sit back and let these wonderful contributing authors steer you toward mysterious lights, mourning spirits, and disappearing hitchhikers as you come along on an armchair ride through the scary side of Texas.

Have you ever noticed the crosses that dot the side of a highway? Each cross represents a memorial for a traffic fatality. Or stopped to read one of the 2,500 Texas Historical Markers placed along a roadside? Others represent even more momentous events that may have occurred under very tragic circumstances, and some of the more infamous ones are mentioned in this book.

When the first explorers came to Texas, they carved trails into the soil with human feet and animal hooves. These early trailblazers journeyed toward the unknown in search of freedom, fortune, and fame. In many cases those early immigrants who came to this untamed land also met untimely deaths due to illness, accidents, and murder. Unfortunately times have not changed that much from the seventeenth to the twenty-first century. And some of the stories that victims have left behind today are as strange as they were back then.

1

Haunted stories are an age-old genre recently rejuvenated by the increased interest of ghosts, and the question as to whether or not they actually exist. Over the past few years an overwhelming number of "ghost hunters" have materialized. Paranormal investigation teams are determined to study ghosts in a scientific manner by using electronic devices such as digital and/or audiotape voice recorders, digital or video cameras, electro-magnetic field meters, and thermometers or infrared thermal scanners.

In this book you will encounter tales of San Antonio's Ghost Children of the Tracks, Port Neches' myth of Sarah Jane Road, and who the Visitant of South Texas really was. Discover the locations of the haunted hangouts in Austin on Congress Avenue, and why a ghostly hitchhiker seeks a ride. Even personal testaments of UFO encounters along Texas highways join the mysteries. It's a journey you will never forget.

I'm certain that some of these stories will give you a rare glimpse of Texas from its birth as a Republic all the way up to present day.

Enjoy your trip,
Joy Nord

Haunting the
Trans-Mountain Highway
by Jacqueline Siglin

El Paso, Texas

The Woodrow Bean Trans-Mountain Highway, or Loop 375, runs through the heart of the Franklin Mountains, connecting northeast El Paso with Canutillo northwest of the city. The road climbs from urban landscape to become a scenic drive through the Franklin Mountains State Park, filled with the geology and desert life of the southernmost end of the Rocky Mountain chain. It is also said to be haunted by ghosts – some of the most dangerous ones in the El Paso area.

The trans-mountain section opened for traffic on August 5, 1969. Soon after that, motorists involved in automobile accidents on the curved four-lane highway reported they had swerved to miss either a man in long flowing robes walking with his dog or a monk with his donkey. The apparitions appeared suddenly, standing in the middle of the road, and then disappeared just as quickly.

Some think their source may be the Lost Padre Mine, another Franklin Mountain story. Hidden from treasure hunters for over three centuries, this lost treasure is surrounded in mystery. In the 1580s Spanish conquistadors and priests moved through the El Paso area on their mission to conquer and colonize the Pueblo villages in what is now New Mexico. One tale says that some 300 burro-loads of silver were left in a mine by Jesuits, who filled in the shaft before they continued on their travels. Another version states that Juan de Oñate, ordered by King Philip II to colonize the upper Rio Grande in 1595, hid 5,000 silver bars, 4,336 gold ingots, nine burro loads of jewels, and four priceless Aztec codices in a mineshaft.

The mission, Nuestra Señora de Guadalupe, in El Paso del Norte, now Cuidad Juarez, Mexico, was established in 1659. While some padres supervised the building of the church, it is said that others crossed the Rio Grande each morning and labored in a gold mine in the nearby Franklin Mountains. The ores from this mine were transported from the mine, smelted into ingots and sent south by burro to the mother church in Mexico City.

For several years things went fine, but in 1680 fleeing priests spread the word south that the Pueblo Indians in New Mexico had revolted against their Spanish conquerors. Alerted to the threat, the priests at the Juarez mission loaded up golden vessels, chalices, and a large store of gold ingots and carried them to the mine. Legend says that it took 250 mule loads to transport all of the treasure. After it was placed in the mine, the padres brought river silt from the banks of the Rio Grande and filled the shaft. The entrance was then covered with rocks so it would look like the mountainside and a lone priest with his faithful dog was left to guard it.

When the Spanish subdued the Indians in 1692, the priests returned to the mission but the mine was never found, perhaps because the padres who knew the location were killed or had been moved to another mission. Over the years treasure hunters who have searched for it have reported seeing a large dog running at them as if to attack.

Does the ghostly monk with his burro and dog continue to maintain his vigil on the newest threat to this treasure, the cars driving on the Trans-Mountain Highway? An anonymous El Paso police officer reports he has heard of, and even taken statements from, drivers involved in accidents on the road who speak of figures seen, figures that force them to swerve their car, and mysterious figures which are never found.

Ghosts of Ascencion Boulevard

by L.C. Hayden

Horizon City, Texas

As the story is told, fatigue encompassed the man named Pedro like a thousand tiny, probing fingers. He glanced at the digital clock mounted on the dashboard. It read 10:07 p.m. Keeping one hand on the steering wheel, he used his other to massage his neck. He wished he were home, but instead, the road before him stretched like a thin gray ribbon set against a velvety black night. Other than his headlights, not a single light lit this deserted road known as Ascencion Boulevard.

Pedro sat up straighter, suddenly alert, almost hawk-like. He made out the image of a lone man, caught in the beam of his headlights. Pedro turned off his lights, then back on, hoping it had only been shadows playing tricks on him, but the ghostly figure ignored Pedro and continued to walk along the roadside.

Pedro rolled down his window. "Do you need any help?"

The phantom turned to face him and then vanished before his eyes.

Pedro has not been the only one to spot this masculine specter as he walks the road heading toward or away from Mountain View High School. Even though he's been spotted several times, no one knows the identity of this phantom or the reason he haunts this road.

This is but one of the many stories associated with Ascencion Boulevard located in Horizon City, Texas, just on the outskirts of El Paso. Even though all of the street signs read Ascencion Street, in legends, the street is referred to as Ascencion Boulevard. Another well-known legend centers on the many bodies buried alongside the road. In the past, people used this deserted road as a dumping ground. In whispered voices, others speak of the Bigfoot-like creatures that also terrorize the area.

Javier Ramirez tells the story he heard from his school friends. A teen and his date went on a quad, a four-wheel all-terrain-vehicle, riding expedition. Because of its isolation, they chose to ride the surrounding flat desert with its low dunes that sit astride of Ascencion Boulevard. She looked forward to riding the quad; he was more interested in sex. When he forced himself on her, she pushed him away. He proceeded to rape her, then to cover his sin, he killed her, leaving her body to rot.

It is said that at the eerie hour of midnight, people riding along Ascencion Boulevard might spot this lonely figure, desperately trying to return home. She finds those who drive the road alone and will sit in the back seat of the car. The driver can see her only through the rear view mirror.

Numerous stories abound about this long, winding road filled with sunflowers, sagebrush, and cactus blooms. Some whisper about the woman who by day is human, but at night turns into a bird and prowls the desert along Ascension Boulevard.

Of all the stories that exist about this haunted highway, none are more touching than the one about a little girl. During the time that Mountain View High School was being built, a little girl was accidentally killed at the construction site. Since then, those riding Ascencion Boulevard can still hear her giggles or at times, her screams of despair. Often she has been seen walking this isolated road, a single figure in the barren desert.

What binds her and other ghostly entities to Ascencion Boulevard, forcing them to stay through eternity, no one seems to know. All that the Horizon City residents know are the stories they whisper to each other.

The Ghost on U.S. Highway 67
by Cecelia Davenport

Girvin, Texas

The supernatural being appeared after a sinkhole ruined a cotton field on the farm in West Texas where my father worked in the late 1950s and early 1960s. My father explained that sinkholes often occur when water pumped to the earth's surface causes underground structures to collapse. What he couldn't explain to me, an inquisitive adolescent, is why a strange figure started flying into and out of that pit in the field.

The *braceros*, agricultural workers from Mexico, labored before daybreak at the farm to siphon water from irrigation ditches into the fields. Like most supernatural beings, the specter chose to be active during the hours of darkness. According to my father, less than a week after the big hole appeared, the Mexican men noticed a bright light hovering near the pit. The bravest *braceros* ran toward the source of the illumination, but the light vanished into the sinkhole.

Their curiosity overcoming their fear, at twilight the same day, most of the workers gathered at the edges of the field surrounding the pit. Almost to a man, they agreed as to what they had witnessed. After all traces of sunlight left the sky, a slender, dark-headed woman, surrounded by light and dressed in a white robe, floated up from the sinkhole and traveled through the air. Paying no attention to the workers, she circled the fields and kept her eyes directed toward the ground. The

9

braceros told the farm manager she seemed to be searching for something.

Within twenty-four hours, the Anglo employees' families, who lived on the farm, had heard the Mexican men's story. People visited the sinkhole during the daylight hours. My father drove his children to view the phenomenon. He explained, as his truck bumped along a rocky road, that the farm's water pumps had created underground havoc. He looked at my youngest siblings, crushed together in the cab of the truck, and put his fingers to his lips when I asked him questions concerning the specter.

Although the sinkhole was approximately forty feet wide and fifteen feet deep, it disappointed me. On the pit's level floor, neat rows of cotton plants still grew, undisturbed by the underground collapse. I peered at its walls for an hour, seeking evidence of a passageway to a subterranean chamber. Perhaps, I thought, the lady in white concealed herself in a cave during the day. I saw nothing but packed dirt.

I tried to talk the only other adolescent in the family, a sister who was three years younger than I was, into hiking with me from our house to the sinkhole after dark to see the lady in white. She reminded me of the time, while chopping cotton, that the two of us had disturbed the resting place of some irritable rattlesnakes and found ourselves performing some serious footwork to avoid being bit.

"I don't want to step on their kinfolk in the dark," she said.

"You're a scaredy-cat," I replied. "I bet you're afraid of the lady, not the snakes."

"I bet you're afraid of her, too."

Later, I discovered my sister was right.

The *braceros*, who continued to see the apparition, remained frightened. My father said they wondered whether the specter intended to harm them. Some of the men believed a *bruja*, a witch, lived in the big hole. They reasoned she couldn't be an angel because she had no wings.

The farm manager, an overworked fellow who was responsible for a large agricultural enterprise, grew concerned when the Mexican nationals threatened to return to their homeland. Orders were issued forbidding any nighttime or daylight visits to the pit. My father warned his children not to discuss the unnatural events with the other youngsters on the farm. If the boss heard any more rumors circulating about the lady, he planned to fire any tale-bearing employee.

In spite of the farm manager's warnings, I overheard a neighbor telling my mother that someone had thrown a wooden cross into the sinkhole. The women said, since the *braceros* continued to see the light enter and leave the pit, they knew the lady in white rejected sin and bad deeds. My mother agreed that crosses drove away evil beings. The Mexican men now believed the apparition was the Virgin Mary, sent to protect them in a strange country, the neighbor stated.

When the woman left, my mother said, "I thought the Virgin always wore a blue mantel over her robes. Your daddy says the men from Mexico are talking about a woman dressed totally in white. I think she's a ghost, not a saint."

"Aren't ghosts kind of blurred around the edges and transparent?" I asked. "Nobody's said you can see through her."

"Maybe new ghosts aren't transparent. They probably generate lots of energy at first. That makes them look solid and helps them to put out lots of light."

The apparition my sister and I encountered on U.S. Highway 67 the year the sinkhole appeared must have been a new ghost.

The fifteen-mile stretch of U.S. Highway 67 that my younger sister and I often traveled as teenagers runs from southwestern Upton County into eastern Pecos County. This two-lane section of the road crossed the Pecos River near Girvin, a village with a population of less than thirty. At night, the darkest section of the fifteen miles lies west of Girvin. My sister and I saw the lady on this part of the highway. We had driven to McCamey in Upton County to attend a beauty contest that evening. After sunset, we started home in my sister's clunker. A mile or two after we passed Girvin I noticed a bright light on the highway's right shoulder.

"What's that?" I asked my sister, shouting over the thumping of the car's engine.

"Somebody spotlighting jackrabbits?"

"Maybe it's goat rustlers. They'll have to work hard to catch the critters." I laughed.

"Maybe it's the lady in white."

As the Chevy moved closer to the light, my sister and I fell silent. Then I screamed, "Step on the gas! It's her!"

The glowing figure illuminated the mesquites and the barbed-wire fence behind her. After what seemed like an hour, we passed the place where she stood. The specter stared into the chaparral across the highway. I hoped she was ignoring us.

"Pray, just pray the car doesn't break down," I hollered as we sped toward the side road that led home.

When we reached the house, we sat in the car until our trembling stopped. Afraid our parents wouldn't allow my sister to drive her old car after dark again, we decided not to tell our mother and father we had seen the lady. They didn't notice our agitation when we stepped inside the living room. Their eyes remained fixed on a flickering TV screen as we walked on rubbery legs to our bedroom.

That night my sister and I stayed awake, our eyes darting constantly toward the window curtains we had pinned shut, waiting for a bright light to shine through the flimsy material. While we kept watch, we talked. We reminded each other the specter couldn't have evil intentions because, even after a cross was thrown into the sinkhole, the *braceros* saw her descending into the pit at daybreak. During the long hours of darkness, we compared our impressions of her appearance.

Even after all these years, a vivid image of the lady remains with me. She stood with her arms crossed over her chest. Short, curly bangs ran across her forehead and the rest of her black hair was twisted into a high knot on the crown of her head. Dark eyebrows, dark eyes, and red lips accented the pallor of her skin, which was almost as white as her clothing. A brooch with clear stones glittered on the bodice of her puff-sleeved, high-necked dress.

The memories of the lady in white belong to people from two different cultures. In northern Mexico today, old men probably tell their grandchildren how the Virgin Mary protected them when they labored as young *braceros* on a farm in West Texas. I respect their interpretation of the events that occurred, but, since I was born into a family whose ancestors emigrated from Germany and Great Britain, my grandchildren hear me say I once saw a ghost on a Texas highway.

Did the Mexican men and two Anglo teenagers see the same apparition? I believe so. Only six miles separate the sinkhole from the section of U.S. Highway 67 where my sister and I spent a few moments we will remember the rest of our days. Traveling that distance wouldn't have been difficult for a spirit with the ability to levitate and soar through the air. An unusual ghost, she didn't haunt one particular place but wandered about the countryside. I believe she was seeking her home and the person who loved her enough to make certain her body was buried with tinted lips, with carefully-arranged hair, and in fashionable attire.

The coiffure and apparel worn by the ghost suggests to me that she died in the decade between 1890 and 1900. By 1890, Girvin existed as a community, and ranching families lived in the surrounding area. Perhaps, before the farm existed, livestock once roamed the same land. Bulldozers clearing fields for the planting of irrigated crops may have destroyed any evidence that a ranch house and a family cemetery once occupied a site where cotton later grew. The collapse of the limestone under the lady's grave may have disturbed her peaceful rest.

After encountering the ghost, my sister and I avoided driving to McCamey for a few weeks. We never saw the apparition again. A year or so after the specter appeared, my father found a job in another West Texas town and we moved away from the farm. I married and lived in Oklahoma for a number of years, losing contact with people in Pecos County who might admit they had seen the lady in white. Now that I live in West Texas again, I sometimes drive, during daylight hours, past the site where the ghost stood. I refuse to drive that section of the road after the sun goes down.

Ghostly Lights of Marfa
by Reba Cross Seals

Marfa, Texas

It was my first date with this tall cowboy, and I was more than just a little bit leery when he suggested we go out and look at the Marfa Lights. Although I was just a freshman at Sul Ross State in Alpine back then, I hadn't just fallen off the back of a pick-up truck. The important "girl talk" that my mother gave to me before I left for college *alone* was of filibuster quality, so I didn't immediately say yes.

Naturally I refused at first, thinking I knew why he really wanted me to ride out that lonely highway from Alpine to Marfa on a frigid November evening. But with the confidence of my young years, I felt I could handle him even if he did turn out to have octopus arms, so I agreed to go. Curfew time at the dorm was 11:00 p.m.; we therefore didn't have much time to get into trouble – or so went my freshman reasoning!

As we chased the last streamers of the day on U. S. Highway 90/67 west of Alpine to about ten miles from Marfa, we soon came to a place where my new cowboy friend pulled off the highway and said, "This is it!" My glance must have told him what I thought of the viewing site, a bar ditch along a state highway!

Pointing in a southern direction, he directed me to be patient and wait. As dusk spread her dark skirts over the cactus, occasional antelope, and distant mountains I was suddenly startled by lights in the distance that appeared where none had been a second before! My suspicious nature, planted my mother's long lectures, made me ask if they could be car lights heading north on U.S. Highway 67 as they neared Marfa. But how does one explain the moving lights that were too far east of that highway, out over the pastures and near the mountains? If they were car lights, they were moving extremely fast over rough ranch roads, and strangely enough, there were no pairs moving together the way car lights do! I was truly impressed and looked at my cowboy date with a little more respect. Well, *some* more respect anyway, as he was still failing our Texas History class.

I remember the lights as mostly white, but sometimes they would be red and orange. But the primary phenomenon to me then, and now, is that they would sometimes quickly bounce up and down above the horizon. The colored lights reminded me of old movie clips teaching one to play the piano and sing songs by following the red bouncing ball over the words and notes. Occasionally two or three lights would merge into one, and then appear to bounce forward, coming closer to us. The distance from us seemed to be a couple of miles.

Since that year several decades ago, when I first saw them as a naive teenager, I've seen and learned a lot more about the Marfa Lights, and have learned to respect them. For one thing, they do not appear on demand, and for another, one cannot predict the quality, length, or power of their show if they do deign to make an appearance. Now as permanent resident of the Alpine area, numerous times I have taken visiting family and friends to the lonely highway area to sit and view the mysterious phenomenon, sometimes in which absolutely nothing happened, and my guests appeared to view me with the same suspicion that I once viewed an innocent cowboy.

Yet other times during the years we have been rewarded with a spectral light show that has been explained in different inconclusive ways by many types of people with various levels of expertise and education. Some suggestions have been phosphorescent minerals in the nearby mountains, swamp gasses (in the desert?), static electricity (which does show up as lightening in time lapsed photos), St. Elmo's fire, car lights or ball lightning, Many others explain the lights in several ways: steep temperature changes common in the area (as much as 60 degrees in 12 hours), UFOs, college students with flashlights, Indian legends, reflective white soil, or simply ghost lights. Numerous groups have come to study the phenomenon for varying length of time, from one day to many weeks with very sophisticated equipment. These mystery lights have been prodded with lasers, dumped upon by planes with bags of flour, chased by jeeps with walkie-talkies, and zapped with radar. But none of these experiments have explained what is visible to the human eye...the lights' ability to divide, merge, blink, change colors, change movement patterns, and vary intensity levels.

The current official viewing site is an extremely nice roadside park built by the Texas Department of Transportation with the research help of a class of gifted/talented high school students from Marfa, Texas. It is well lit at night, clean, and conducive to sitting for hours if necessary waiting with photography equipment for the exciting experience. I've wondered if my cowboy friend has ever returned to the area with his family to tell the same story of the night we saw the rampaging Marfa Mystery Lights. Cars frequently line up along the parking lot and people visit amiably with strangers, each hoping to see something occur that is as yet scientifically unexplained or paranormal as some believe. And definitely the lights do not show up every night on cue to the disappointment of many passing tourists who just stop by the viewing site on their way to the rest of their lives.

The only common denominator seems to be a night sky, but they have appeared at dawn and dusk. The Marfa Lights appear on calm nights and during thunderstorms, often having their photographs taken with lightening flashes. They have appeared in snowy Decembers and on a blistering 4th of July. They are more visible on dark new moon nights, but can also be seen during a full moon.

The earliest recorded mention of the lights is by a rancher named Robert Ellison in 1883. During World War II a huge army airbase occupied this exact location. Between 1942 to1947, thousands of men passed through the base. American and Allied pilots alike were once stationed on this desolate land. Recent reports claim that army cadets were taught to fly within sight of the mysterious Marfa lights as part of their training. However civilian skeptics question why the bizarre lights were not publicly mentioned during this time. Speculation is that this knowledge was kept secret by the military so panic would not breakout during wartime. Even today, military pilots who observe UFO sightings are strictly discouraged from telling the public.

Many reputable and professional citizens of the Marfa/Alpine area, as well as notable visitors from around the world have given creditable eye accounts of what they have seen. As a retired school teacher, a Sul Ross State University adjunct, and a current monitor of alternative certification teachers and principals, I often tell my first-hand experiences to people, which usually makes them laugh or roll their eyes. For many years now, I've lived among the rugged peaks in the southern end of the Rocky Mountains, and nowhere else have I seen dancing lights than beside U.S. highways 90/67. *My* favorite explanation for them is that they are the remaining campfires lit by old Apache Chief Alsate who once hid high up in the nearby Chisos (ghost) Mountains as signal lights to help his people once more find their way home.

The Sad Tale of Cry Baby Bridge
by Mitchel Whitington

Dekalb, Texas

This story started back when I was a teenager, more years ago than I want to add up, in the wonderful East Texas town of Hooks. One of our favorite activities was "riding around" – that is to say, piling in a friend's car and driving from one end of town to the other, then back again. We'd stop at the Dairy Queen just to see who was there, maybe see if anyone was hanging around at the church, turn around on Precinct Line Road, and start the circle all over again. Conversations ranged from how the football team was going to do on Friday night to where the bass had been biting the most out at Texarkana Lake. It was a fantastic time – and place – to be a kid.

I remember one night vividly, although I'm not exactly sure when it took place. I think that it must have been in the fall, because the weather was just chilly enough to run the car's heater on low. A couple of us had been cruising around and we stopped to get a cola and see what was happening at the DQ. No one was there at the moment, but it wasn't long until a carload of friends showed up and ordered a basket or two of fries to munch on while we visited. In the course of conversation someone mentioned having gone out to "Cry Baby Bridge" in DeKalb the week before. She said that it had frightened everyone so badly that they'd practically flown back to Hooks, pushing the speed limit for all that their car would go.

"What is Cry Baby Bridge?" someone asked. "Did you see something that scared you?" another guy joined in. "Where is it?" still another fellow asked. Everyone was chattering at once. The girl who'd brought up the topic just sat back and smiled, waiting for the questions to subside.

When we were all sitting there on the edge of our seats, she began her story: "Twenty or thirty years ago a woman who lived out in the countryside around DeKalb was coming home from the store. She had her three babies – triplets – in the back seat with the sacks of groceries. The lady ran into one of her friends at the store, and they stood in the aisle and gossiped for almost half an hour. Of course, she realized that her husband was going to be coming home from work to an empty house, so she quickly checked out and started home. She didn't want him to be mad because his dinner wasn't ready, so she was driving much faster than usual to try to beat him home. When the car rounded the corner right before a little country bridge, the rear end started sliding and she over-steered to compensate. By the time the woman got to the bridge, the car was hopelessly out of control, and careened over the side and crashed into the creek. Someone found her unconscious behind the wheel about an hour later. They rushed her to the hospital in Texarkana, and although the doctors fought hard to save her life, the lady passed away. Right before she died, she looked up at a nurse and asked, "Are my babies all right?" The nurse immediately notified the County Sheriff that there might have been infants involved in the wreck, and the officers scoured the creek bed for the rest of the night. They pulled the car out, of course, and even got volunteers with hunting dogs to assist in the search. The bodies of the three infants were never found."

She stopped her story, and looked around at her audience. We were all sitting there in rapt attention, and even in the normal din of the hamburger joint, you could have heard a pin drop. Taking a deep breath, the girl continued the story. "People forgot about the wreck over the next few years, until two cars met at the small bridge on a summer evening. Since only a single car could fit safely on the bridge, one driver honked his horn three times to get the other fellow's attention to wave him on across. Now, since it was so warm, both cars had their windows open. As one slowly eased over the bridge, there was the unmistakable sound of babies crying in the night. The drivers stopped and looked over into the creek bed, but the only thing that was there was the tiny stream trickling under the bridge." Our storyteller's voice dropped to almost a whisper. "That's how it started. People soon realized that if you stop on the bridge at night, turn off the engine, and honk the horn three times, you will hear the crying voices of the three tiny babies who were never found."

Now, there is absolutely, positively, no way on the face of the Earth that you can tell a story like that to a group of teenagers and not anticipate the response. Everyone uttered the same words in unison: "Let's go!"

The remaining French fries were wolfed down, the colas were drained, and we all piled into one car. To this day I can't imagine how nine or ten of us managed to cram into a modest sedan, but we did. It was a short drive over to DeKalb, and the girl who'd spun the story for us was giving directions: turn left here, slow down and turn right, look for the next road, and so forth. I will never forget the sight of the headlights cutting through the night, and eventually hitting a small bridge on a dark, lonely, country road. "That's it," the girl whispered.

The fellow who was driving stopped the car on the dead center of the bridge, and we slowly rolled the windows down. "Kill the car," someone said, and when he did, the night was deathly still. He pushed the headlight control, and we were then parked on the bridge in total darkness. For a moment, while we were waiting for our eyes to adjust, it was like being in some kind of sensory deprivation chamber. "Do it," I heard someone whisper from the back seat, and suddenly the three loud retorts of the automobile's horn split through the night.

Like I said at the first of this chapter, which was more years ago than I really want to count up, I remember it like it was yesterday. When starting to write this account of Cry Baby Bridge, I launched a huge research campaign to uncover the facts of this story. I was immediately overwhelmed with the information that I found. Consider just a few of the stories:

"The story of Cry Baby Bridge takes place in Union County, South Carolina. Just before you get to the historic Rose Hill Plantation, there is an old bridge with rusted steel frames at the top. The local legend has it that if you park on the bridge and cut off your car, that you can hear a baby crying and then see the mother looking for it. One day in the 1950's a woman threw her baby off the bridge to spite her abusive husband, and she has been doomed to walk the creek in search of her child."

"One rainy night in Oklahoma on a small dirt road, the story behind Cry Baby Bridge was born. A young woman was leaving home to head for work, with her small baby safely strapped into the car seat. When she crossed the small wooden bridge, the dam on the lake next to the road suddenly broke from the pressure of a rainy season. It wiped out the bridge, and swept the car downstream. The mother's body was found washed up on the lake's shore the next day, but the baby's body was never found. Local officials dragged the lake and the stream, but never found the baby's body. The bridge is still washed out to this day, and it is said that if you go there on a rainy night you can still here the baby cry, and the frantic mother will appear and ask you if you have seen her baby."

"A number of people have heard the story of Cry Baby Bridge here in New Hope, Pennsylvania. The accident took place at least fifty or sixty years ago. Legend has it that a woman became pregnant with twins, but after the babies were born the father wanted no part of the new family. With no

husband, and no way for her to support herself or her children, the young lady decided that it would be best if she took the lives of herself and her children. She carried both of the babies out onto the bridge, climbed over the side, and plummeted herself and her children to their deaths. The people who have been out to the bridge have walked near the center and heard the cries of what sounds like two screaming infant children coming from below, near the water."

"Cry Baby Bridge is a place in Faison, North Carolina that is truly haunted. It all started when a woman and her baby were going home from church one late, rainy night on Highway 403. The lady was driving across the bridge a little fast when her car slid and plunged into the river below. Both the mother and the tiny baby drowned. Some people say that if you go to the church, ring the doorbell, and run back to the bridge, you will soon hear a baby crying beneath the bridge. If you do hear the baby cry, then your car will not start – you will see a greenish glow in the water, which is the spirit of the baby watching you. Your car will not start because the infant wants you to help him and his mother."

"Cry Baby Bridge is located in Genesee County near Flint, Michigan. There was once a young, practicing Satanist woman who had given birth to a bastard child. She thought that she could gain power into the spirit realm by sacrificing her baby's life to the Devil. One night she placed the baby on a railroad trestle next to a cemetery, and lit two white candles. The baby was then hit and killed by a passing train as it crossed the bridge. Now, if you go there in October during a full moon, and light two white candles, you will hear a baby crying and see a ghost train passing by in the night."

"In a little town named Doylestown Ohio, a pregnant woman was driving to the hospital to have her baby back in 1963. The baby came before she could get there, and she had to stop and give birth on a small country bridge. While holding her tiny baby, she became distraught over the fact that the

father had left town months before, and threw the newborn over the bridge. She couldn't get the final cries of the baby out of her mind, so she went down to the train tracks near the bridge and stood there so the train would kill her that night. As the story goes, if you go to the bridge at Midnight you can her the baby softly crying, and some people have even seen a ghost train going by on the tracks."

I could go on and on with the stories that I found about "Cry Baby Bridge," from one coast to the other, and from Canada down to Mexico. The story is apparently an urban legend that has been spread to small towns across America – my version was one that was based in DeKalb, Texas, but it could have just as easily been anywhere else. I should have known – when I was telling someone at school about my experience at Cry Baby Bridge, they lit up like a lantern and said that they'd already been there, a week before. When they started telling me where it was, though, their bridge had been on the opposite side of town from the one that we visited. It was an urban legend in the making, way back in the 1970's.

So what happened to all of us in the car that dark, fall evening? Well, I hesitate to tell you now, especially in the light of the many Cry Baby Bridge stories that I found. Through the still of that night, however, when the last blow of the horn was echoing off of the trees around us, everyone in the car would probably swear to this day that we heard the cry of a baby – the imagination is a fantastic thing. The driver fired the car to life, sped away, and we rode back to the Dairy Queen with a mixture of screams and howls. Back under the bright florescent lights, with a cold cola and order of fries in front of us all, we laughed and accused and doubted and dared. It was wonderful being a teenager back then.

Naked Lady on Hwy. 385

by Reba Cross Seals

Marathon, Texas

In the early seventies, when living seemed easier and more relaxed, a strange thing happened one summer evening in west Texas. My husband and I drove from Fort Stockton with our young children to meet friends at The Post in Marathon for a Saturday night picnic and dance. The Post, a well-known family party site, is an old watering hole of beautiful natural springs. Remnants of an old army post known as Fort Pena Colorado still remain.

Thirty years ago everyone took their children with them most places, and The Post was a magnet for families. Everyone watched everybody's kids frolic in the pond, catch fireflies, drink too many sodas, eat too much junk food, and generally have a great time. Everyone looked forward to the outdoor parties and dances.

My family, consisting of my husband and myself, two young boys, and our little girl Kimberley, left our home in Fort Stockton and drove south on U.S. Highway 385 for about eighty-five miles until we saw the Santiago Mountains which stretched toward the Rio Grande River. After crossing U.S. Highway 90 in Marathon we drove another five miles south to the park. We spent the late afternoon picnicking and tossing breadcrumbs to the ducks by the pond. At dusk the dancing began on a large concrete slab to live music, with country and

25

western as the prevailing beat. And all the while adults were watching out for the young kids who were often on the dance floor. Mamas taught their sons how to dance at The Post, and little girls, like my daughter Kimberley, waltzed around on her Daddy's boots.

Sometimes we took our pickup camper to spend the night camping out at The Post, and then we put the kids to sleep inside when they were sticky-dirty and tired to the point of crying with their eyes already closed. And the adults kept on dancing.

But late one night for some unremembered reason, we had gone to Marathon in our car instead of the pickup camper, and had to return to Fort Stockton that same night, about 1:00 a.m. in the morning. With the kids asleep in the back seat, we drove about twenty miles north of Marathon on that little traveled U.S. Highway 385 when something strange happened.

It was a bright, moon lit summer night when all of a sudden our headlights picked up a figure running toward us from the bar ditch on the right side of the road. It was a naked woman, fairly young, waving her hands, screaming, and trying to stop our vehicle. Automatically, my husband Robert (Robo) Cross-started to slow down, but fear gripped my heart.

"No, no, don't stop! It might be a trick," I screamed. "There might be men waiting in the bushes to jump out! Don't stop, please don't stop!"

Frightened that there might be Mexican nationals with a dope shipment (not unheard of in that area) or some kind of desperados hiding to way-lay a car, I was frantically concerned for our three children asleep in the back seat. Robo agreed to drive on, but insisted that we alert the sheriff in Fort Stockton when we got home.

But that's not the end of the story. Just a few years ago, my oldest son, Justin Cross, who is now grown and has a young family of his own, was visiting at a party with a Marathon friend named Ben Ramirez. The men started swapping stories as men do at a party, and Ben said, "You know, the strangest thing happened years ago when I was a kid. My mom and dad and my brothers and I were on our way to Fort Stockton late one night when a naked woman ran out in front of our headlights and tried to stop our car! But my mom yelled, 'Don't stop! *Cuidado*! Don't stop! Drive on! It's a trap!' So we drove on."

I have no way of knowing these many years later if it was the same night, or maybe it happened nightly for a while. I only know that the sheriff and his deputies never found anyone out there on lonely U.S. Highway 385, and no one ever reported a woman missing.

To this day I ponder on the old fort, remembering that it was built back in 1879 to protect settlers and ranchers from marauding Indians, and I think of the west that was "hell on horses and women." Are there really such things as restless ghosts who wander the area? The fort was abandoned in 1893, leaving the springs once again unprotected. Do ghosts still stay around because the springs were a dangerous oasis for centuries? Did anyone ever help that poor lady? I still wonder whatever happened to that naked woman on U.S. Highway 385!

27

Road to Del Rio

by Billie L. Stephens

Del Rio, Texas

This story was related to the author by E. Thomas, a local contractor who installs Mexican floor tile for a living.

On a hot August day I drove down U.S. Highway 277 toward Del Rio to pick up a load of ceramic floor tile from Mexico to use in my business. I usually stayed in the area for four or five days per trip.

As I drove along, I started to nod and could feel my eyelids start to get heavy with fatigue. Knowing the Texas summers, I usually left the house around five in the morning to get most of the trip done before it really got hot in the afternoon. However on this particular trip, I hadn't been able to get to bed early the night before. The kids needed my help to buy and pack their summer camp gear, and then I had to pack my suitcase and truck for my own trip.

I finally got to bed around midnight, but then the dog started howling at the moon.

The neighborhood noise, the bugs around the porch light and everything that moved kept me awake. The dog, afraid of her own shadow, would bark all night to make sure anything in the night knew she was awake and watching. Finally, after I got up and locked her in her kennel, I went to sleep about one o'clock.

On the road, I shook my head, turned up the radio and turned down the air conditioner, hoping the noise and the cold would help wake me up. After a couple of miles I could tell it wasn't working and I either had to stop for a nap or risk ending up in a ditch.

Then I saw a hitchhiker up ahead walking down the road in the direction I was going. I thought if I gave him a ride, I would have someone to talk to as I drove along.

The answer to keeping me awake.

I slowed and stopped next to the guy. "Going to Del Rio if that's where you're heading," I offered. He was dressed in faded jeans and a western shirt, his hat pulled low over his face. What I thought was a bag, turned out to be part of a saddle.

"Mighty obliged," he stated tossing his saddle into the back of my truck. He climbed into the passenger seat and offered his hand. "Name's Buddy, and yep, I'm headed to Del Rio, or right the other side anyway."

"What are you doing walking so far from anywhere?" I asked.

"Wrecked my truck a ways back and just took off walking. I was coming back from the rodeo over in Pecos and got a few days before the next round so thought I'd go see Mom for a couple of days," Buddy answered.

Now I did not remember seeing any wrecked truck on the road or any other vehicle for that matter. Those roads were usually pretty deserted most of the time. But then again I had been nodding and might have overlooked it.

Buddy turned out to be a perfect traveling companion. He talked and had an opinion on just about every topic we discussed. When we got to the subject of scripture and the gospel, he monopolized the conversation. I would have thought he was in training for the ministry, not the rodeo. It was like he had memorized the Bible and quoted scripture line for line. During our talk, I held my own since I served as a deacon in my church and had taught Bible classes for the last twelve years. We really raised the roof on my old pickup truck.

Finally I asked him about his rodeo riding. He talked a little about roping and bull riding. When I asked about his horse, he got quiet. Then he said his horse had been badly injured in the wreck and had to be put down. He seemed real sorry about losing his horse because he was silent for a while as though remembering the events of the accident.

"How long ago did this wreck happen? Were you hospitalized for a while?"

"A little while ago," Buddy replied. "I spent a couple days in the hospital before I left."

Now that got me to thinking. If the wreck had happened a few days ago that would explain why there wasn't any truck or horse trailer alongside the road. However, he didn't talk as though he had just been released from the hospital. Someone would have driven him home instead of him hitchhiking. Things just didn't add up.

The truck cab grew quiet once again. Buddy seemed lost in his own thoughts, and I wondered why some folks would not even bother to go and check on their children while in the hospital.

After about ten minutes I thought I would ask him about his wounds and the next rodeo so I looked over to the side. My passenger was gone. I almost jumped from my seat. I then checked the rear view mirror to see what had happened to the young man. I didn't see him anywhere.

My truck doors automatically lock when the truck gets up to ten miles per hour, so I knew the doors were locked. I had not heard them unlock, the door open, or anything else. All I knew was the young man was no longer in the truck.

I pulled over to the side of the road and stopped. I walked around to see if his saddle was still in the back. The bed was empty. I knew that if he had bailed out he couldn't have gotten his saddle out with him.

You can bet your bottom dollar that I didn't sleep the rest of the trip to Del Rio.

That young man's visit stayed with me the entire trip, and to this day I think about it every time I drive down there.

Author's notes: I checked out Thomas' story about the young ghost hitchhiker. It seems that about twenty-three years ago there was a young man driving back from a rodeo in Pecos. He had done quite well and was going to visit his folks who lived down around Del Rio. The young man fell asleep while driving home about three in the morning. He ran off the highway and totaled out his truck and his horse trailer. It killed the horse and mangled the young man who lived about thirty minutes after he arrived at the hospital. If driving the road to Del Rio be on guard for the young cowboy who goes by the name of Buddy.

Could it be that Buddy may have accompanied Thomas to save his life, seeing how fatigued he was?

Unsolved UFO Sightings at Levelland
by Joy Nord

Levelland, Texas

Perhaps the most active period of UFO sightings in U.S. history happened in Texas during November 1957. Throughout that month, the U.S. Air Force acknowledged more than 400 reports of unidentified flying objects.

The initial sightings occurred in Levelland on the evening of November 2, when dispatcher A. J. Fowler, the officer on duty at the Levelland Police Department, received fifteen similar telephone calls from panic-stricken citizens reporting UFOs in the area.

The first call came in around 11 p.m. from Pedro Saucedo, a thirty-year-old Korean War veteran and local farm worker. Mr. Saucedo told Fowler that he and his friend, Joe Salaz, had been driving in his truck on State Highway 114 when they saw a big flame to their right.

Saucedo said, "Suddenly the truck engine stalled, and the headlights flickered off. Just as I got out of the cab, a large yellow and white thing, about two hundred feet long and shaped like a torpedo, roared over my head. It was so close that I could feel the fiery blast of its engines, moving at about six hundred to eight hundred miles an hour."

A certified statement made by Saucedo also states: "I thought it was lightning. But when this object reached my position it was different. It was so rapid and had quite some

32

heat that I 'hit the deck' because I was afraid. I called to Joe but he didn't get out. The thing passed directly over my truck with a great sound and rush of wind. It sounded like thunder and my truck rocked from the blast."

Once the object had disappeared, Saucedo climbed back in the stalled vehicle. He inserted the key in the ignition and the engine started without a difficulty. Since the object seemed to be traveling east toward Levelland, the two men went in the opposite direction to Whiteface, a small community about fourteen miles west of Levelland, where Saucedo phoned the police.

Fowler first thought Saucedo was drunk and dismissed the report as a prank call.

Although he logged it, he didn't take any further action. However, an hour or so later when he received a phone call from Jim Wheeler, the dispatcher took the ex-soldier's report more serious. Mr. Wheeler had also been driving on State Highway 114 four miles east of Levelland, when he came across an egg-shaped object sitting in the middle of the road. "As I slowed down, my car sputtered to a stop and the headlights dimmed. When I climbed out of the car to get a better look, the luminous, greenish-blue object rose about two hundred feet and then vanished," Wheeler said. When he got back in his car, the engine turned over without a problem.

During the next few hours, Deputy Fowler's telephone lines became bombarded with reports very similar to those encounters described by Mr. Saucedo and Mr. Wheeler.

The dispatcher decided to start logging the calls after he heard from Jose Alvarez, who was in Whiteharral, eleven miles north. He had also encountered a strange light that had killed his car engine for a short time.

Deciding that something unusual was taking place, Fowler alerted several police officers on patrol and the county sheriff. After he relayed the reports, he continued to manage the phone lines.

At 12:45 a.m. Officer Fowler received a call from Ronald Martin, a frightened eighteen-year-old truck driver from Waco, who was just northeast of Levelland on Oklahoma Flat Highway. He told the officer that his engine and headlights suddenly failed when he approached within two hundred feet of a brilliant, egg-shaped object "glowing like a neon sign." As he got out of his truck, the UFO quickly shot straight up with a roar and streaked away. The truck engine and headlights worked perfectly when the object vanished.

By this time Sheriff Weir Clem and Deputy Pat McCulloch had driven to Oklahoma Flat Highway to investigate what had provoked all of the commotion. As the officers cruised down the road, a large, glowing, egg-shaped mass appeared about a thousand feet south of them. Sheriff Clem said that this strange craft rose from the field and headed their way. When the object approached his truck, the engine died and the headlights went out. The sheriff jumped from his vehicle and flattened himself on the ground as the thing soared over them with such force that it rocked the truck. Immediately the officers radioed headquarters and learned that two state troopers, Lee Hargrove and Floyd Levin, stationed at nearby Littlefield had also witnessed the same object several miles behind the sheriff. Later, in a signed statement, Trooper Hargrove said: "I was driving south on the unmarked roadway known as the Oklahoma Flat Highway and was attempting to search for an unidentified object reported to the Levelland Police Department. That's when I saw a strange looking flash, which looked to be down the roadway approximately a mile to a mile and a half... The flash went from east to west and appeared to be close to the ground."

Unlike the civilian witnesses, the state troopers did not experience any problems with their vehicles when they saw the object. But the Levelland Fire Marshall, Ray Jones, who was also searching for the UFO stated that his car's headlights dimmed and the engine sputtered but did not die, just as he spotted a "streak of light" north of the Oklahoma Flat.

In the meantime, thirty-two miles east of Levelland, authorities in Lubbock monitored radio traffic. A reporter for the *Avalanche-Journal* heard about the sightings and called the Levelland Police Department to inquire what was going on. Dispatcher Fowler told the journalist, "The telephone has been ringing off of the hook. They are driving us crazy. All of the callers seem upset by what they have seen."

Following several more calls, Officer Fowler telephoned the Lubbock Police Department and Reese Air Force Base, located west of Lubbock. The officer on duty at Reese said none of the base's aircraft had been flying at the time of the sightings. Also, the Civil Aeronautics Administration of the Lubbock operation claims it had not been tracking any planes in the Levelland area at the reported time of the multiple sightings.

The following day, a swarm of newspaper reporters from across the country and other interested parties converged on Levelland, eager to write about the startling activity of the previous night. The Sunday edition of the Lubbock newspaper printed a dozen paragraphs about the sightings, written in the early morning hours. However, The Associated Press rewrote the story and distributed the article to its clients, which caused national publicity for the sightings.

Not everyone who witnessed the strange object reported it immediately. Newell Wright, Jr., a nineteen-year-old freshman attending Texas Technological College in Lubbock, was on his way home to Levelland at 12:05 a.m. on State Highway 114 when his car engine began to sputter about nine miles east of town. He claimed that the ammeter on the dash jumped to discharge then back to normal, and the motor "started cutting out like it was out of gas." He let the vehicle coast to the shoulder of the road, and the headlights dimmed and went out seconds later. He got out of the car and raised the hood to check the battery. Finding nothing wrong, he slammed the hood. When Newell turned to get back into his car he noticed a bluish-green oval-shaped object, flat on the bottom, and about 125 feet long, sitting on the road farther down the highway. He stated that the body seemed to be made of an aluminum-like material, but no apparent markings or other details were seen. Frightened, he got back into his car and hoped that another vehicle would come by. None did. As he observed the object, it rose almost straight up and then vanished in an instant. When he tried to start his car, it was fully operable. "I then proceeded home very slowly," he later said, "and told no one of my sighting until my parents returned home from a weekend trip...for fear of public ridicule. They did convince me that I should report this, and I did so to the sheriff around 1:30 p.m. on Sunday afternoon, November 3."

The sightings were investigated by Project Blue Book, a research group created by the U.S. Air force in 1951 to investigate UFO reports. The investigators interviewed only three witnesses – Saucedo, Wheeler, and Wright. Hearing that thunderstorms were present in the area earlier in the day, the Air Force team concluded that a severe electrical storm was the major cause for the sightings and reported automobile malfunctions. In their report, they attributed the sightings to "a ball of lightning." The Air Force did not interview any of the other witnesses, nor were they mentioned in Project Blue Book's final report. Naturally, we all know that a ball of lightning does not land on roads and disrupt car engines; in which, this case is perhaps the most accumulative of vehicle interference ever recorded in the United States.

Despite the government's findings, two prominent UFO researchers, Dr. James E. McDonald, a physicist at the University of Arizona, and Dr. J. Allen Hynek, an astronomer at Northwestern University, disputed the Air Force's explanation. Both men argued that no electrical storms were in the area when the sightings occurred. UFO researcher Antonio

Rullan published a detailed analysis of the Levelland sightings in 1999. Further examinations of various weather records and the competing claims of the Air Force, Dr. McDonald, and others compelled Rullan to conclude, "there was no severe thunderstorm in Levelland during the time of the sightings... there could have been a few clouds with light rain in the area despite no rain being reported at the nearby Lubbock weather station." Rullan also stated, "Conditions for scattered lightning, however, cannot be discounted as lightning conditions did exist."

In *The UFO Experience* Dr. Hynek wrote "In terms of probabilities, that all seven cases of separate car disablement and subsequent rapid, automatic recovery after the passage of the strange illuminated craft, occurring within about two hours, could be attributed to coincidence is out of the statistical universe – if the reports are truly independent, and they are, according to the tests we've used throughout."

Just one hour before the first Levelland sightings, the Russians had launched their second satellite into space with a dog named Laika on board. Coincidence? Who knows, as this unbelievable case is still unsolved.

Who Screamed?

by Carol MacDonald Menchu

Electra, Texas

What happened on that little wooden bridge north of Electra many years ago to cause the area's citizens to be absolutely sure that the bridge is haunted? This most likely explanation has something to do with a woman named Sheila.

Could it be that because the road is so far out and away from anywhere there were very few witnesses to any of these happenings... except, perhaps, the witch burning? And was Sheila burned as well as hung? Did she, does she, still scream?

Conjecture would have it that this portion of the road was closed down before whatever happened on the bridge happened. That certainly is possible for the 1920s event and the 1980s event. Could that be because the rancher who owned the surrounding land fenced it in to keep his cattle safe? Could be.

The best directions send us eight to ten miles North of Electra, Texas on State Highway 25 to Wolf Road that is beyond Valley View. Then head east to where it intersects with Moeller Road. Going north on Moeller, the road becomes overgrown with grass and weeds and there is an electrified fence across the road. The road is public and if you are careful to refasten the fence so as to keep the rancher's cattle in, you can drive through and go on to what is left of the road to the Screaming Sheila Bridge.

The other set of directions says that the bridge is five miles west of the Clara church, on Wolf Road. There may be back roads from the ghost town of Clara; however they are not on the Texas map. You can follow Highway 240 to Moeller Road and turn north continuing until you reach and cross Wolf Road.

One tale about the bridge says that in the mid-1800s a girl named Sheila was put on trial for witchcraft, found guilty, and burned alive on the bridge, and the perfectly burned circle indicates where it happened. People also said you could hear her screams during the night.

Another story says that a woman named Sheila was hung off the side of the bridge, swinging out over the river as she gasped for her last breath, but doesn't mention 'burning' and doesn't mention 'screaming'.

Still another story goes that in the 1920s a woman found to be cheating on her husband was tied up, beaten by him and eventually set on fire. While her husband and his friends looked on, she went up in flames, which burned the hole through the bridge, dropping her burning body into the creek. There were no stories about her screaming connected with this, but is it possible her screams are the screams heard?

Then there are the high school kids who claimed to have had a party on the bridge in the 1980s and accidentally set it on fire. Only kids screaming and yelling here and no one burned or hurt.

It still remains: Who was hung? Who was burned? But, more importantly, who screams?

The answer may never be known... this bridge keeps its secrets well.

Anson Ghost Lights

by Tammy Petty Conrad

Anson, Texas

In Anson, a small town outside of Abilene, in Jones County, residents and sightseers have discovered a mystery in their own backyard. Traveling east on U.S. Highway 180, the Mt. Hope Cemetery is 1.7 miles from the U.S. highways 83/277 and 180 junction. Visitors will tell you that once they drive down the unpaved road that passes by the cemetery, they turn around at the crossroads and stop, turning off the engine. Within a few moments, those who flash their headlights three times are given a vision they don't quickly forget.

The white light appears in a variety of ways. Sometimes slowly moving towards them, at other times it moves from side to side, almost erratically. It has been seen up amongst the treetops and it varies in size and sometimes even color. It can even be more than one light at a time. Anyone brave enough to venture in its direction only finds that it just disappears. The only sound that accompanies this spectacle is from the visitors, most likely gasping or praying for deliverance!

The explanations of "who" or "what" is responsible for the appearance are vague and vary depending on who's telling the story. They all revolve around a mother looking for a lost son or sons. Most say that the woman lived in the area sometime in the 1800s and had given her child or children a signal, flashing a lantern three times, to use if there was trouble. Some say it happened as late as the Depression in the last century. Whenever the trouble occurred, she has been left forever searching.

One story claims, a mother sent her three boys outside to chop wood one evening, and were told them if they encountered any trouble, they should flash their lanterns three times. They did. But by the time their mother reached them, the boys were dead. Another story states that during the Great Depression, a young boy wandered away from home on a cold winter night. His frantic mother searched along the road holding aloft a lantern to light her way, but she never found her child. A different version has an older son who is a railroad worker and signals his mother from the train as he passes. But the saddest version is the one about a son being sent to look for the family Christmas tree never to return. In this story, the worried mother went out to search until she too succumbed to the elements. It is said she is buried in the cemetery and that's why the light of her lantern appears at three flashes of light. She is once again searching for her beloved son.

I couldn't help wondering who she was as I searched online for the names of those interred there at the cemetery. Was she Anna E. Kennedy whose son William died at five years old? This woman lived for over 30 years after her son died. Or Mollie B. Yates whose son Lewis died at twelve years old? It seems we will never know the exact story.

Of course there have been "investigators" who have surveyed the location and tested to determine that it is nothing more than the lights from cars on the nearby highway. Local law enforcement authorities don't tolerate loiterers in the area since they too think it is only car lights. Believers dispute that and have done their own tests with no such results.

I myself am not brave enough to make an evening visit. But I would be curious to search the grounds and read the tombstones to find any clues about the mystery woman. Would she rest in peace if we could discover what happened to her family? Is it a cruel joke we play to flash our car lights raising her soul from a fitful rest, only for her to discover that once again her son or sons are nowhere?

What is really happening in that lonely cemetery besides local high school students or area college co-eds being scared out of their wits? Maybe you'll need to investigate for yourself. Don't forget your camera!

Three Ghosts of Keys Crossing
by Janelle Fears

Brownwood, Texas

A short distance from Brownwood three ghosts are often seen kneeling and throwing roses into Indian Creek, a tributary of the Colorado River. A tribe of Comanche, who came to this area around 1740, camped along this creek in the 1800s. This region is in a very remote, unpopulated part of Brown County where one of the most bloody Indian battles took place. Frontier family members were also killed on this site, and it is felt their spirits haunt the road to the creek. History implies these spirits originated from Indian an legend or curse.

Local stories say that persons who drive on this road at night should proceed slowly, or they might flip three times and be severely injured... or even die. While that is merely a legend, when traveling down the road, people have definitely seen shadowy figures staring through brush and trees.

Penateka, meaning honey-eaters, were the Comanche who frequented the Brownwood vicinity and were well known for their trading, horsemanship, and kidnapping of children and women settlers. Everything they traded was stolen, but relatives of captives would trade with them trying to buy back their family members, stock, and other valuables. Since Apache, Jumano, and Pueblo Indians already lived in the Southern Plains, Comanche had to be fierce fighters in order to

43

drive other competing tribes from the region during their migration south to Kerrville and Austin.

My husband and I interviewed some campers named Josh, Bridget, and Raymond who were familiar with local ghost stories and Indian legends. They validated the story of the Keys Crossing ghosts, but said they had not seen them personally. The three interviewees were natives of Brown County, and camped with their parents and siblings for years at Keys Crossing, and then later with their own children.

Indian Creek was very shallow and the campers' children were playing in the rocky creek bed. We drove across the creek in our truck to the opposite bank where the group's campground was located.

Approximately ten years ago a family member brought their pet German shepherd with them to Keys Crossing. He disappeared for a while and then came back into camp with a human toe in his mouth. This was extremely unnerving to them, but they never reported it to the police. Josh, Bridget, and Raymond all declared this story to be true. Bridget said the local ranchers do not like people driving along the creek because Indian artifacts may be present on their land.

Originally, Keys Crossing had an island in the middle of the creek, which is probably why it was called Keys Crossing. The island was removed, possibly for flood control. Cherokee and Comanche were the primary tribes found near Brownwood and Abilene. The Potawatomi tribe was a branch of the Cherokee. Josh said his great grandfather was a member of the Potawatomi, and he passed down the stories of the Indian campground and battle. In 1869-71, the Potawatomi tribe was allotted land for a reservation in Oklahoma near the Kickapoo. Josh's great grandfather was on this reservation.

Many believe that the three ghosts of Keys Crossing may be spirits of those killed in the Indian battles of the 1800s.

The Screaming Bridge
by Mitchel Whitington

Arlington, Texas

When I was researching haunted roads, the name "The Screaming Bridge of Arlington" caught my attention immediately. I was sure that a place with such an interesting moniker would be worth looking into. As it turns out, the story of Screaming Bridge is a tragic one, and the events were very real: racial hatred, a horrible car wreck, and many lives shattered.

To begin with, the name "Screaming Bridge" was given to a small, one-lane bridge that crossed the Trinity River on old Harrison Road (now known as Davis). Its name came from the fact that the bridge was so old that when a car crossed, the timbers would creak and moan, as if the bridge itself was screaming from the strain of the weight. A resident of Arlington who grew up not far from the bridge, told me, "It was just a thrill ride over a very old bridge. I was always wondering if it was going to collapse while driving over it. It never did, of course – it just sounded really spooky."

On the other side of the bridge was an area of town known as Mosier Valley. The community was established in the 1870's by emancipated slave families, most of who were freed from the Mosier plantation. The Trinity River bottomland was given to the freedmen by the Mosier family, and the African Americans established a close-knit farming community

45

there. To get to Mosier Valley from Arlington, one would first cross Screaming Bridge, then a smaller bridge just before a railroad track.

The 1960s was a very turbulent time in our nation's history; there were individuals who were violently opposed to any integration between races. A few such individuals set fire to the smaller bridge before the railroad track, probably assuming that an accident there would deter any African-Americans from coming into Arlington from Mosier Valley. Hatred always clouds the mind, though, and what the individuals failed to take into consideration was that many people, regardless of race, frequently crossed the bridge. According to my source from the area, "Driving out north of town down the dark country roads and crossing over the Screaming Bridge was pretty much all there was to do for teenagers in those days."

The railroad discovered that the bridge had been burned out, and posted warning signs on both sides. Someone removed those signs, however, so that there would be no notification to drivers that the bridge was gone. On an evening in February of 1961, six teenage girls were out cruising after seeing a drive-in movie in Fort Worth – three girls in the front seat, three in the back. My source remembered the accident well, since she attended Arlington High School with the young people involved. "The kids had gone over the Screaming Bridge and were headed towards the railroad crossing. The girls did not know that the smaller bridge was out until they got right on top of it. The driver tried to gun the motor to jump over the bridge onto the railroad tracks. They did not make it, and drove head-on into the embankment on the other side. The three girls in the front seat died. One of the girl's fathers was an Arlington police officer who was sent to investigate the accident – he had no idea that he would be the one to find his daughter dead. It was a horrible thing to happen. The three in the back seat were injured, but survived the wreck."

46

It was a tragedy for everyone involved. The perpetrators of the bridge-burning finally stepped forward and took responsibility for the death of the girls. They were three Senior boys from Arlington High School, along with another young friend, and were expelled from school and not allowed to graduate. A reward was posted for the people who removed the signs, but they were never identified.

There are many legends that are floating around about Screaming Bridge, and most start with the idea that the wreck occurred on the bridge, and involved two cars. From there, some of the tales are:

- If you stand on the bridge and look down into the water, the date of the accident and the names of the girls who died will be on glowing tombstones in the river.
- Sit in the middle of the bridge on the anniversary of the night of the accident, and at midnight a heavy fog will rise up from the river and you will see headlights approaching the bridge.
- Go to the bridge on the accident's anniversary at midnight, and the wreck's sounds will be reenacted – although there are no cars to see, if you look down at the river you will see the ripples in the water as if an automobile just splashed in.

The legends around Screaming Bridge seemed to have evolved out of the long-ago tragedy. The tales told by teenagers grew over the years, until they now bear no resemblance to the original event, since the accident didn't happen on Screaming Bridge, but instead on the smaller, burned-out bridge beyond it.

As to the fate of the original Screaming Bridge, my source said, "I never heard the stories they are telling about the Screaming Bridge – that had to have happened after my school days. When I was in school it was shut down because it was too old. The bridge had to be rebuilt, and now it is not even there anymore. You can't get to the site because the city closed down the road and built an alternate route to the Hurst-Euless-Bedford area. You can see the place where Screaming Bridge was from afar if you know exactly where it used to be. Also, the bridge where the six kids went off trying to cross the railroad tracks has been closed – you cannot get to it either. The new road that was built takes you away from that site."

The ghost stories of Screaming Bridge illustrate why it is important to examine the history of a haunted location. Occasionally, you will find that the actual facts on which the stories are based are flawed, which may be an indication that the associated haunting may be nothing more than a campfire legend.

I don't mind that the Screaming Bridge ghost stories aren't true – when looking for spirits, it's just as important to identify the false reports as it is the true ones. My biggest regret is that the bridge isn't there anymore. I'd love to drive slowly across it one night, just to listen to the creaking and crackling that gave the bridge its name, and maybe let a little chill run up my spine.

The Dublin Sighting
by D.C. Campbell

Dublin, Texas

Among the beliefs that Laura Schneider held that night in 1980 was the importance of working for her family and spending time with them on special holidays. A dedicated mother, she balanced work and family. It was no surprise that she worked on Christmas Day, and then left immediately afterwards to take her family to Ft. Worth for the holidays. They packed their presents and treats, and headed north. As they drove on U.S. Highway 377 toward Dublin, she had no idea that she was about to add another experience to her life – one that would take her thirty years to allow to be told in print. That night, Laura and her family experienced the existence of unidentified flying objects.

Her husband accompanied Laura and their two sons; all were wide awake in anticipation of fun times ahead with their Ft. Worth relatives. At 10 p.m., it was a cool, crisp night with clear, starry skies. Traffic was light, given that most people were already at home or their choice destinations for Christmas.

Suddenly, huge lighted objects filled the sky ahead of them. These massive structures were unlike anything they had ever seen before. Built the size of cruise ships five stories tall, with brilliant lights shining from portholes lining the entire length of the crafts, they floated slowly southeast in single file barely above the tree tops. Shocked and in a daze at what they were seeing, Laura and her family pulled off the road so that they could watch the space ships as long as possible. They gazed up into the portholes, bright enough and large enough that if anyone looked out, they would see the face.

No one looked out.

Laura had her family turn down their windows to hear the sounds.

Except for the Texas winds blowing softly through the trees, a total eerie silence. No jet sounds, no mechanical sounds. Nothing. Just three spaceships floating in absolute silence. And as Laura and her family continued to watch in wonder, the ships picked up light speed momentum and vanished into the skies.

Laura and her family were not afraid, just in total awe at the magnificence of what they had just witnessed. The sheer size and the brilliance of the lights left them in shocked silence for a few moments before all four were able to talk again and acknowledge that they had just experienced a UFO sighting.

And what took Laura and her family thirty years to tell her story? Maybe because they now have more company than they initially thought during the skeptical 1980s. An Associated Press poll reports that fourteen percent of Americans, more than 40 million, said they had seen a UFO at least once. Reports of sightings have skyrocketed in the past twelve years. On a Saturday night in January 2008, five hundred people crowded into a building in Dublin, close where Laura had had her experience, to tell and hear of UFO sightings. More than two hundred sightings were recounted that night, some going back thirty years. The witnesses in Dublin filled a broad spectrum: a former Air Force historian, a police constable, a trucking company owner, and the Dublin police chief. One man, a businessman and pilot, described his sighting as a mile long and a half a mile wide. He said it was larger, quiter, faster, and lower to the ground than any airplane he'd ever seen. Sounds familiar, doesn't it?

And just in case you think Laura's sighthing was an isolated incident, think again. Major sightings were also reported in the same area for three days after Laura and her family became UFO believers on that Chrismas night.

Sinister Holloman's Road

by Robert Fears

Mesquite, Texas

Holloman's Road, once a narrow graveled lane on the southern edge of Mesquite, completely vanished without leaving any evidence that it had ever existed. A creaking windmill and an old white frame house remained for a while after the road disappearance. Today, a concrete foundation is the only sign of previous inhabitants.

The dark, sinister road, mostly hidden by a dense cover of trees and brush, meandered between Lawson Road and Cartwright Road. From Cartwright, Holloman's road ran between what is now Berry Middle School and a new housing development. The road's previous entrance off of Lawson Road is blocked by an established subdivision.

And for many years, there were ghost stories associated with Holloman's Road.

It is not known whether the Holloman's Road specters still remain and fight for their privacy. These apparitions might have been souls of people who met hideous deaths on Holloman's Road, seeking revenge before they continued their journeys into the hereafter.

During the 1960s, the Klu Klux Klan held meetings on Holloman's Road during which they burned crosses, chanted hate-filled rhetoric, and supposedly executed enemies. Years later, screams pierced the night air on several occasions and when people tried to investigate, the disturbing sounds moved just ahead of them as they walked across the property. Fire pits full of human bones were said to have been discovered, only to disappear by the next day when authorities were guided to the site.

As long as there was access to the road, spirits discouraged its use. People anonymously reported bullets hitting their cars with no indications of where a gun was fired. Tires were punctured without any obvious cause and vehicles became stuck when it had not rained. One car caught on fire, was quickly consumed in flames and within seconds, the only remaining part was a charred frame.

The 1981 murder of a beautiful, thirty-year-old woman and her five-year-old son brought more apparitions to Holloman's Road. An abandoned 1978 tan-and-blue Ford Thunderbird was discovered on Holloman's Road by Dallas County Deputy Sheriff, Roy Baird. Deputy Baird found a women's purse and gloves in the front seat of the car and wrapped Christmas presents, personal papers, and a blue canvas bag with white trim in the back seat.

Upon further search, Baird found Kristopher lying on his side 137 feet directly north of Holloman's Road. He was wearing a blue coat and pants and had been shot in the forehead with a single .38 caliber bullet. Roxann lay approximately three feet from her son, shot once in the cheek and again in her temple. She was covered from head to toe with a green blanket and, like her son, was fully clothed. From the position of their bodies, detectives felt that Ms. Jeeves was forced to watch her son's execution before she was killed.

During the autopsy, Dallas County chief medical examiner Charles Petty found bruises around Roxann's neck and 100 cubic centimeters of blood in her abdominal cavity. From this evidence, investigators surmised the killer may have choked Roxann into submission and then pinned the woman to the ground with his knee as he shot her.

Car registration papers showed Ms. Jeeves to live in Apartment 234 at a complex called The Sussex Place on Larmanda Street in northeast Dallas. During interviews with other residents, detective Larry Forsyth learned that a black male was seen leading Kristopher by his hand toward the parking lot. The man appeared to be about five-foot nine-inches tall, weighing approximately 180 pounds and in his early-to-mid thirties. He wore sunglasses, a dirty white T-shirt under a blue jogging top and light brown pants covered with greasy smears. He wore his black hair cut short.

Don Crawford, who worked in a gas station near the Sussex Place, phoned the sheriff's department within hours of the murder. He said he had pumped gas that morning for Roxann Jeeves. He remembered Ms. Jeeves sitting at the wheel of the Thunderbird saying nothing except, "Fill her up." A black male sat quietly next to her in the front seat.

The case soon grew cold and wasn't solved until 2003. New DNA testing helped convict a Texas inmate, George Hicks. At the time of his conviction, Hicks was 52 years old.

After this awful crime, Holloman's Road became even more eerie and developed a mystical aura. Traffic on the road increased primarily due to people's curiosity. Several reported they became overwhelmed by a sense of dread. Others felt they were being watched, even in broad daylight. One person reported that men in black capes jumped up and down on his van.

Teenagers dared each other to walk down the road at night. It was reported that some disappeared and have never been found. The City of Mesquite finally built fences across the road's entrances to stop traffic.

An anonymous visitor climbed over one of the fences to gain access to Holloman's Road during the early 1990s. As he walked along the road, he felt a spirit attach itself to him. He still sees and hears things that aren't there and when he tries to sleep, he sees brutal murders being committed.

The spirits of Holloman's Road definitely did not want to be disturbed. Did they vacate the area when new development moved in or will they haunt the new residents?

Horse Thief Gulch
by Carol MacDonald Menchu

Waco, Texas

Lindsey Hollow Road has had a reputation of being haunted for more than a hundred years. Many paranormal experiences along the road have been reported. People claim they have felt paralyzed, heard disembodied screams, and seen spectral apparitions.

Legend claims that the ghosts of two brothers haunt this lonely, shaded road. In 1880, the Lindsey brothers were suspected of stealing horses and possibly some cattle, also. Exactly where they stole the livestock, and who they stole from, is never mentioned.

However, the location in which the brothers were killed was probably somewhere in McClennan County, west of Waco and south of the Brazos River.

Over the years several versions of this story have been fabricated, which leaves the truth dangling at the end of the rope along with the Lindsey brothers.

One story, according to late historian Roger Conger, a group of lawmen were taking the brothers to trail in Waco for stealing the horses. Unfortunately for the Lindsey brothers, vigilantes ambushed the group in the bluffs and hollows along the Brazos River. The attackers shot the brothers and then lynched them up. The tree used to hang them is in a hollow about hundred feet from the roadway in what is now the Cameron Park area.

Allegedly the lawmen were in on the plan and they conveniently stayed out of the line of gunfire, which makes them no better than the vigilantes. People say they can still see the shadowy images of the brothers' hanging bodies from an old tree in Lindsey Hollow. Other people have heard loud pops that sounds like gunfire, and moans.

One legend becomes two when it seems the Lindsey brothers were being chased by ranchers for stealing horses over and around the bluffs south of the Brazos River. These ranchers supposedly followed them into a hollow and proceeded to shoot both brothers. Afraid of being arrested for murder, so the story goes, the ranchers buried the brothers in the hollow.

Why then, the hollow would be named Lindsey Hollow if no one but the ranchers knew the brothers were killed and buried there becomes a mystery in itself, although it does explain why the ghosts of the brothers had been seen in the Lindsey Hollow area.

Two legends become three when it seems ranchers in the Waco area were having problems with cattle thieves and ended up cornering the Lindsey brothers. One rancher shot one of the brothers and then, while they were headed into Waco with the dead body and the live brother, another rancher shot the second brother. Again, afraid of being considered murderers, the ranchers supposedly buried the bodies in a hollow.

Of course, this legend takes us back to the question, why was the hollow named Lindsey Hollow if no one but the ranchers knew the brothers were killed and buried there? It also remarks of the brothers' ghosts being seen at different intervals by different people.

Lindsey Hollow Road and Cameron Park are located in Waco, Texas. To find the general area you can leave I-35 at Exit 335A (Fourth and Fifth Streets) and go West on Fourth

Street (one-way) to North Spring Street. Turn left on North Spring Street to Fifth Street. Turn right on Fifth Street and it becomes Lindsey Hollow Road until it reaches Baker Lane. From there, stop and listen for gunshots and moans...

Need Some Help?

by Lance Nord

Oakwood, Texas

This story was told to the author by a truck driver known only by the CB handle *Grumpy*.

On June 27, 1982, I geared up early for the next day's haul from Arkansas to Texas. That morning me and some other men from a hay farm loaded up hundreds of square bales onto my forty-eight foot flatbed to haul down to Hondo, located west of the Alamo City. When I pulled out and got rolling I thought by all means, this should be an easy run, since I didn't have to drive through the Big D or the Dome. And if I timed my arrival just right, I'd hit Capital City while all the four wheelers were still asleep.

After driving for several hours, I stopped in Naples at the local choke and puke for supper and asked the waitress to refill my favorite blue thermos with strong black coffee. It was going to be a long night. By 10:45 p.m. I steered onto Highway 79 south headed toward the "big road," Interstate 35, in Round Rock. At night that strip of Highway 79 is always quiet since most people around those parts live off the land and when the chickens sleep, so do they.

About fifteen miles south of Oakwood, I decided to switch off the CB and turn on the radio to listen to some country music and sing along. When I glanced down to adjust the knobs, I noticed the time read 1:30 am. I knew it was late because my body told me to pull over and stretch my legs. That's a nice way to say it's time to water the tires.

I spotted a nice gravel area where I could stop. When I slowed down, I saw movement up ahead. I couldn't tell what it was. I set the air brakes and hit the high beams. The light revealed a man walking toward my rig about 200 yards away. I thought to myself, "Boy! Am I glad I pulled over when I did 'cause I could've hit him."

The fellow had an unsteady gait, weaving around like he'd been into grandpa's old cough medicine; but the sight of drunks out late wasn't new to night truckers. I dimmed the lights, and jumped out to walk around the back of the rig to take care of business. I knew I'd be back to the cab before he could get too much closer. After I checked the rear lights I headed up front on the passenger side. At the nose of the rig, I lit a smoke and took a good long drag. The man came closer I could see he still had trouble with his balance. While I contemplated the pros and cons of taking another drunk home, I finished my cigarette. I opened the cab door and turned to look at the fellow one last time.

At this point I could see he wore in a pair of jeans, work boots, and a white t-shirt. Stained with blood. I threw hesitation to the wind and ran over to him.

"You ok? Hey son, do you need some help?" I asked.

Blood trickled from his forehead. He looked dazed and smelled like a brewery.

"Yes sir, I think I do." His voice shook and I could barely hear him.

I gently took his arm and led him back to my rig. I grabbed some clean rags I kept for emergencies. He took one of the rags and started to sob. Meanwhile I took out an old blanket to cover the seat. With that much blood, I wanted to avoid a clean-up mess later.

"Let's get into the truck son, and I'll take you over to the hospital. I opened the door of the cab and told him to watch his step. Unsteady as he was, he might fall. No sooner than the words left my mouth he banged his shin on the fuel tank step. I knew it must have hurt something terrible 'cause those steps leave ugly bruises that can ache for days if you hit them the wrong way. He didn't even whimper, but swayed while I tried to help him regain his balance. After what seemed like forever, he finally sat in the seat. I shut the door, hopped down, ran to my side and got in. The interior lights revealed the poor boy was a mess. The large, jagged gash on his head supplied a steady stream of blood down the side of his face. His hair, plastered down, looked black and shiny. The next town was several miles away where I could get him some help.

I got back on the road as fast as I could and went the same direction he walked from. "Son what happened to you?"

"I swerved to miss a dog, and ran off the road up there in that big cornfield."

I reached for my thermos, thinking it wouldn't hurt to get some coffee in him, and managed to hand him a cup of the nasty stuff. He sipped at it and seemed to breathe a little easier. As we neared the cornfield, he pointed to a wide flattened swath visible in the distance. "We need to stop. I have to check my car."

"No, son we've got to get you some medical care. That's a nasty cut you got on your head and looks like it's going to need some stitches." I felt bad for him, and thought that the car was probably a lost cause anyway. He got real agitated and put his hand over the door handle, like maybe he'd jump out. Alarmed, I continued to glance between him and the road, trying to decide what to do.

His voice dropped even lower when he said "Please sir, I'll need to get my wallet. All my stuff's in there."

That made sense in view of what would be ahead of him, with all the hospital paperwork and police reports. I slowed down. "Okay, let's make it quick though. The sooner we get

61

you to town the better." I eased off the road and stopped where the corn had been flattened.

In his haste to escape my rig, he spilled coffee on the dash as he fidgeted with the door handle.

"Whoa, there. Wait a second, and let me get my flashlight." I rooted under my seat and grabbed it. When I got around the side of the truck he was standing next to the headlights waiting for me. I turned the light on and started to make my way across the shallow embankment into the corn. The path made by the car was bumpy and uneven where the stalks had bent at different angles. He walked to my left, slightly behind me, shaky.

"Are you sure about this?" I asked. "I can always go on ahead and get it for you while you wait in the truck. Won't take but a minute."

He shook his head and kept walking with his head down. I shrugged and kept going.

Silently we followed the car's path, which seemed like a long walk. The night seemed darker than usual since the moon wasn't out, and the cornstalks seem to whisper as we passed through them. Except for the crunch of stalks, there were no noises, not even the chirp from a cricket. The further we went the colder it got. I shivered as a chill ran down my back. I wished I'd put on my jacket.

About a hundred feet in, I started to wonder if we were going to find the car. Then I spotted it jammed against a utility pole with the front end curved around it on either side. I caught the scent of gasoline, and the closer I got, it smelled like a hot engine. I swung the light toward the front of the car, and saw another person's silhouette slumped over the wheel. Why hadn't the injured guy told him that someone else was still in the car? Shocked, I hollered and ran toward the car at full speed. I forgot everything else as I tried to see in. This looked bad.

My heart pounded. Out of breath, I leaned over and shined the light over the backseat and up to the front where the driver sat motionless. I jerked on the handle, but the door didn't budge. My adrenaline pumped so hard I yanked and the door finally screeched open. I leaned in and gently put my hand onto the injured boy's shoulder. He fell back, and his head flopped lifelessly. The light hit him full in the face.

I froze. Goose bumps marched over my entire body. Speechless, I looked behind me for the man I had driven here, thinking this had to be a twin brother. There was no one around. Scared spit-less I shined the light around wildly, still unconvinced. Once again I looked at the boy in the car, and tried to make sense of it all. His vacant eyes stared into space. The gash on his head was in the same spot as his passenger's. His clothes were the same, a bloody t-shirt, jeans and work boots.

Then I saw my old rag I'd given to the guy I picked up – clutched in the dead man's hand.

I screamed and jumped back and fell on my butt. The flashlight bounced out of my hand and went out. I scrambled to my feet in total darkness. I tried to guess the direction I had come, but panic made me lose my senses.

Cornstalks surrounded me and pressed close, and for a second time, they seem to whisper at me as I ran through them like a madman. My heart pounded as I searched for the road and the safety of my truck. I mumbled a prayer and desperately pushed aside stalks of corn. I fell to my knees, out of energy, out of breath and more scared than I'd ever been in my life.

Finally, I saw headlights, and broke through the field, right on the edge of the road. My truck was up ahead and the headlights glowed like a beacon. I took a deep breath and half ran, half stumbled toward my rig.

I sat in the driver's seat for a few minutes and tried to rationalize what just happened.

Was I losing my mind?

On the dash sat the half empty coffee cup where the young man had left it. I didn't want to touch it but needed to remove it before I drove off. With trembling hands, I grabbed the cup, it was ice-cold and the coffee frozen.

Without further hesitation, after I dropped the cup, I turned over the engine and got out of there like the Duke boys of Hazard County.

A few short miles away at the next town, I stopped at a convenience store.

Ironically, a police car was there, with two officers making a coffee stop. I went in and told them I saw a car go off the road a few miles back. When I gave them the location, the cops glanced at each other.

"Don't worry about it," said the older cop. "We've heard this story more times than you can shake a stick at."

I didn't tell them the whole story. They wouldn't have believed it anyway—or maybe they would have. I still had me some miles to go so I jumped in my truck and sped off with my hay, anxious to make my delivery and get back home to Arkansas as fast as I could—by any other route but this one.

Walking With Sarah
by Joy Nord

Donahoe, Texas

In 1978 the Texas Historical Commission placed a marker near the Donahoe Community, located on Donahoe Road, two miles north of FM487, seven miles east of Bartlett in Bell County, Texas. The marker reads: "Colonists settled in the late 1840s along the fertile Donahoe Creek. Samuel Gibbs Leatherman (1799-1888) arrived in 1854 and opened the first mercantile store. He gave land for the cemetery and brought in the first doctor. In 1880 Leatherman donated land for the schoolhouse. It also served as a church until 1911 when Thomas Jefferson Jones and his wife gave this site for the Baptist Church. Donahoe boasted a town square, post office, telephone system and voting precinct. With the coming of good roads to other towns Donahoe declined, leaving only the cemetery."

Both the town and the creek were named after a merchant who explored the area during the Texan Santa Fe Expedition of 1841. During the late 1840s settlers acquired land along the creek. According to the 1860 census few people lived in Donahoe. After the Civil War in 1865 the population started to increase. By the late 1880s, the town had sixty residents. The Science Hill School was the only school in Donahoe. It served the town's children plus the surrounding area. In 1903, one teacher had seventy-nine students. Throughout the years, residents of Donahoe have either died or moved away so that by the late 1970s, the town had been abandoned.

Today an old windmill, scattered farm implements, and the cemetery, all within the compound of private land, are the visual remains of the once thriving community. Yet stories that tell of buried treasures, and submerged bodies beneath the Blackland soil, keep Donahoe alive.

Several hundred yards down hill from the community cemetery on the eastside of Donahoe Road a wrought iron fence protects the roadside grave of Sarah Herndon, which exists the same way she died – alone.

In 1863 Sarah Herndon (age sixty-three) drowned while trying to cross the Donahoe Creek. Legend claims that her cries for help can sometimes be heard during the night along Donahoe Road, especially near the bridge.

The story passed down through generations tells that Sarah left her home one evening to go visit the Daniel McKay family. Although she had taken the same route many times, this would be her last. She didn't know that the recent heavy rains and loose sand had caused quicksand to form. While she walked along the swollen creek, soft sand stuck to her shoes. Suddenly her feet became embedded in a liquid sandpit. She struggled to free herself, but the hem of her long skirt started to float upon the murky waters. Sarah was sinking. In sheer panic, she kicked her legs and then thrashed her arms working against a vacuum left behind by the movement. As the force of nature pulled Sarah down into the bowels of Donahoe Creek, she screamed for help. But none came.

When Sarah did not arrive at the McKay home, the family organized a search party.

Despite the community's immediate efforts to find their friend, Sarah's body did not resurface until a few days later along the creek bank. Apparently she had taken along her knitting, because when her body was found she had a sock still clinched in her hand. Sarah's badly decomposed body was not in any condition for a proper burial. Hurriedly, the men who found her dug a grave just far enough away from the receding waters of where her remains were found.

Located at the bottom of Donahoe Hill at Jones Crossing, by the creek, Sarah's grave has survived more than 145 years. However between January and February of 2008, Sarah's headstone was vandalized and is no longer there. The original marker read: Mrs. Sarah Herndon – Born 1800-Died 1863. An index finger pointing heavenward was chiseled near the top of the stone.

According to an article printed in the *Temple Telegram* in 1973, another story claims that the screams along Donahoe Road come from an old woman who disappeared around the same time as Sarah Herndon. The author wrote: "Years ago on an old mossy wooden bridge crossing the Donahoe Creek between Vilas and Bartlett, it was reported that the shrill voice of an old woman could be heard calling out to people passing over the bridge. The folk history behind the mysterious midnight voice goes back to the time when a woman crossing the creek became entangled in the mud-laden waters until the mud completely entrapped her. Her body is still captured beneath the murky layers in a grave of mud."

Whether or not the ghostly wails along Donahoe Road are fact or fiction, Sarah Herndon was a real person who drowned in Donahoe Creek. Although her family has not lived in the area for more than 100 years, her grave is always maintained, and flowers are forever present; however no one seems to know who the overseer is of Sarah's final resting place.

In 1989 the Texas Historical Commission placed a marker at the Donahoe Cemetery, located 200 yards west of Donahoe Road, two and one-fourth miles north of FM-487, seven miles east of Bartlett, Bell County, Texas. The marker reads: Established in the 1860s by pioneer settlers Samuel G. and Helen Leatherman, this cemetery served as the community burial ground for citizens of Donahoe. The earliest documented grave here is that of the Leatherman's infant grandson, who died in 1869. Other interments include those of an unidentified woman and child who died while traveling through the area; pioneer settlers and veterans of the Texas Revolution, the Civil War, and World War I. The cemetery remains as the only physical reminder of a once-thriving community.

The "Ozone" Road
by Robert Fears

Oakalla, Texas

Maxdale Road starts at the Lampasas River and extends westward to the central Texas community of Oakalla. Through the years, it has been dubbed the "Ozone" because residents and visitors experience hallucinations and encounters with ghosts.

After reading many accounts of these experiences, my wife and I became curious and decided to visit the area. On a bright, crisp fall morning, we drove from Georgetown northwest on State Highway 195 through Florence. Approximately ten miles south of Killeen we turned left onto Ranch Road 2670 and followed a narrow, winding road over cedar covered hills until intersected Maxdale Road. Confused about the exact location of Maxdale, I stopped and studied the area. To my left down a gentle slope, I saw an old metal truss bridge spanning the Lampasas River. We drove to the bridge and after further examination, I realized we were at the infamous "Ozone" Bridge and the "Ozone" Road.

As we stood looking down through tall pecan and cottonwood trees into a deep, dark ravine that had been cut by the river, we couldn't help thinking of recorded encounters with ghosts. One story pertains to a man who was unable to save his lady from drowning in the flood-swollen Lampasas, so he hung himself from one of the bridge trusses. Apparently if

69

you walk onto the bridge on a certain night and at a certain time and shout "Mary" you might hear footsteps of someone running toward you and see red, glowing eyes. Others have seen a ghost wearing jeans and a white tee shirt. People claim if you stop your car on the bridge, turn off your headlights, count to ten, and then turn them back on, there will be a man hanging from a noose.

At least two different versions are told of a school bus running off the bridge. Some say, the driver had a heart attack while crossing, and as a result, lost control. Others say a truck driver failed to give right-of-way on the one-lane bridge and both vehicles plunged into the river. Everyone, who tells these stories, agrees that the driver and all children aboard the bus died in the river. Some say, heavy footsteps and moans mark the driver's presence. Others imply that when you walk onto the wooden-floored bridge, and are quiet and listen; you will hear cries of screaming children. Before the bridge was condemned and barricaded from automobile access, people claimed that if you stopped on the bridge and put your car in neutral, you would hear children telling you to hurry and get across to the other side. They would then help push your car across. Today, people suggest you park at one of the barricades and then dust the top portions of your car with baby powder. They further suggest you walk onto the bridge and stand quietly for a few minutes. Soon you will hear children's voices and crying. Upon returning to your car, you will find children's hand and foot prints in the baby powder.

We walked halfway across the bridge, stopped and peered into clear water of the Lampasas as it flowed rapidly over beds of shiny, white gravel. We were awed with the area's natural beauty but certainly did not see or hear anything out of the ordinary. Then all of a sudden, a large white-tailed buck bearing huge antlers came bounding out of the trees like he was being chased by demons. He ran down the bank into the river, half jumped and half swam across, and then charged up the opposite bank into a grove of trees. He disappeared as quickly as he appeared. Luckily I had taken two snapshots of the frightened creature as he swam across the river.

We crossed to the other end of the bridge hoping to see signs where the deer had passed, but to no avail. On this end of the bridge, people have seen flickering lights moving in haphazard patterns over the river. When car lights are turned on, the eerie flickering lights disappear for a few seconds and then reappear.

There is a bronze marker encased in stone that gives a brief history of the bridge.

Before a bridge was built, people forded the river where water was shallow. When the river flooded, crossing was impossible and people became marooned on the west side.

According to the marker, Bell County Commissioners Court approved construction of a bridge in July 1913 to provide residents of Maxdale reliable access to Killeen. Before it was completed, however, the bridge was destroyed in a flood. The commissioner's court contracted with Hess & Skinner Engineers to build the bridge a second time and it was completed in 1914.

We walked back across the bridge, still seeing no sign of the deer. We got into my truck, took a new bridge across the Lampasas, turned left onto Wolf Ridge Road, and stopped at a cemetery. We learned that some of the cemetery's graves date back into the 1860s. It is rumored that this cemetery contains a witch's grave and when there is a full moon, her headstone glows a shimmering orange color like refection of flames from a fire. A legend tells that she practiced black magic and caused the death of a rancher. She was captured by some local citizens and hung without a trial. Just before the horse on which she sat was given a smack on its rump, she pronounced a curse upon the town.

Maxdale, founded in the 1880s, established a post office in 1883. A year later the town had twenty citizens, two churches, a school and a cotton gin. By 1914 the population had increased to fifty and a general store had opened. The post office closed in 1926, but three businesses and two churches remained until 1948. In 1990 the population had deceased to four. Today, one church remains along with some rural residences and the Maxdale Cemetery. According to various sources, one of the original caretakers, who walked with a limp, haunts the cemetery along with the witch.

To finish our trip along "Ozone" Road, we took Maxdale Road (FM 267) into Oakalla. This long, winding road has numerous sharp curves, hills and bridges and is a road on which many people have died. Ghosts of some of the dead are said to haunt this road on a regular basis. Headlights of a truck will just appear from nowhere and chase you till you run off the road. People have reported various strange feelings while driving this road at night such as hair rising on the back of their necks, chills, and visions of medics tending to injured people. Fortunately we drove the road during daylight and did not experience any of these feelings. Maybe someday we will get enough nerve to visit "Ozone" Bridge at night and then drive "Ozone" Road back to Oakalla in the dark.

Trolls of Joppa Bridges
by Janelle Fears

Joppa, Texas

The legend of trolls under the Joppa Bridges are vague and, and are possibly a mixture of local folklore and hoax. Still, the stories have been part of the local culture for years.

What we do know is that people hear noises of creatures breathing heavily and making weird sounds from under the bridge. At night those who have waited patiently are rewarded with the running of the "trolls." Actual sightings seem scarce to support this tale, but many have heard the haunting sounds and have let their imagination run with the trolls.

The very small town of Joppa, Texas (population 34 in 2000) is seven miles northeast of Bertram in Burnet County. Originally it was named Pool Branch, after a nearby pool formed by a waterfall. Pool Branch was renamed in 1891, after securing a post office. Inhabitants agreed on "Joppa." The name comes from biblical reference of "Jaffa" which is currently a seaport in Israel. Another interpretation in the biblical sense is "beauty and comeliness."

The first Joppa businesses included a blacksmith, mill, and cotton gin. Later development of school and church buildings in 1881 on the north side of the river came about with two acres of land being donated by J.S. and Jane Danford.

Two bridges were built across the San Gabriel River in the late 1800s. It is not known which bridge was built first, but the bridges are known as Bridge I and Bridge II. Bridge I can be easily crossed by coming from Bertram via Bear Creek. When you see the Bear Creek Cemetery sign turn left on RR 270 and follow until you arrive at Bridge I. Continue past Bridge I and at the three way intersection of RR 200, RR 272, and RR 210 you will find Bridge II. Bridge II is within a few steps of an old church.

The two bridges seem identical in their architecture. Both cross the San Gabriel River and were still used as late as 1989. New bridges were built alongside the original bridges sometime around 1990.

The San Gabriel River is deep and narrow in this location and considered to be a favorite fishing spot for locals. The river is heavily treed in both bridge locations. Even on a bright day, it tends to be shady and dark in and around the bridges. Bridge II has ropes hung from the bridge and surrounding trees that are apparently used for swimmers trying to cool off on hot, summer days. We saw an unusual sight under the newer bridge. A dead bird seemed to be hanging precariously from the underside of the bridge possibly ensnared in a spider web. The web was not visible, so it seemed the bird was in mid air with no support.

There are many interpretations of the word troll, which comes from Nordic literature and Scandinavian fairy tales. Generally the word is used to describe mythical giants and/or a smaller sized race with oversized ears and noses. The Scandinavian fairy tale "Three Billy Goats Gruff" has achieved international recognition, and in modern fantasy literature, trolls are featured to the extent of being stock characters. In the United States and Canada, the old belief in trolls is likened to a more modern belief in Bigfoot and Sasquatch. Trolls are mentioned in English, Germanic, European, and Middle Eastern literature.

Fairytales featuring trolls were popularly written in the late 19th century to early 20th century, reflecting the romanticism of the time. Tales of trolls were never meant to be true or real, but were used to explain unusual happenings. Troll characters never looked particularly human in form. Bridges and trolls seem to have a secure place in fairy tales and modern day legends. Although it is not known how long the stories of the Joppa Bridge trolls have been in circulation, there is no question that the tales are still told today.

Baby Head Mountain
by Billie L. Stephens

This story was told to the author by David Towers.

After living on the east coast for several years, I had the opportunity to move back to Texas in 2000 when the company I worked for got bought out by a larger corporation.

On Friday evening, as the work week drew to a close, I would pack up and drive to my aging parent's home near Comanche. I took the roundabout way out of Austin so I would miss the rush hour traffic and end up headed north on State Highway 16.

After a few trips I grew interested in the countryside. Sundays, on my way home, I would stop along the roadside and read the historical markers. It made the trip more interesting as I was never in any hurry to get back into the hustle and bustle of Austin's traffic.

One marker particularly caught my attention. It was about an Indian raid in the 1850s that resulted in a baby being kidnapped, then slaughtered and the body left on top of a mountain in Llano County. This later became known as Baby Head Mountain located approximately ten miles north of Llano on Highway 16.

According to the marker, family and friends searched the area but never recovered the head. On doing some research I heard different stories. One story claims that just the baby's skull was found. While others stories claim the opposite, the body but not the head. Another version tales that a search party discovered the dismembered body of a missing child. Her head impaled on a stick near the summit of the hill. All versions of the story were weird and had me wondering what really happened and what the parents of this infant felt and did.

I kept up the weekly trips and enjoyed getting to know my parents once again, and able to say "I did" rather than "I wish I had" gotten to reestablish family ties.

As the weeks passed I forgot about the baby except when I passed the Texas Historical Marker.

One weekend I decided to take off work a little early. I packed me a few sandwiches to eat at the little roadside park about half a mile past Baby Head Mountain.

The spot was shady and right off the road so it wouldn't delay my trip. But, I'd piddled around the house and left later than normal, and by the time I researched the roadside park it was beginning to get dark. Since it doesn't take much light to eat a sandwich, chips and soda, I stopped anyway.

The traffic on State Highway 16 is minimal, especially around suppertime. I sat on top of the picnic table with my back to the hillside and facing the highway. While I ate supper, I studied the scenery. Across the road was a small mountain, trees and what looked like a creek on the other side of a small pasture. Nighttime overtook, the landscape faded into darkness. Suddenly a chill crept across my back and the hair on my neck stood up. I jerked around and stared at the brush and trees but didn't see or hear anything.

Weird.

I turned halfway so my back wasn't directly to the woods and continued my meal.

Then, once again, a cold chill ran up and down my spine, making me spill my soda.

Normally darkness, and being alone, doesn't bother me. In fact, I've often thought the dark was my friend and companion.

77

Now I heard someone walking toward me through the brush. At first I thought it might be a cow, or a smaller animal such as a raccoon or armadillo. Although I couldn't make out a shape or where the sound was actually coming from, I know it was getting closer. And of course I didn't have a flashlight with me.

I stood up, put the remains of my supper back into the bag, and then turned to face the brush. By now it was quite dark, just a sliver of moonlight hung from the sky. I watched the brush as I walked backwards to my truck. The thought of being attacked by mountain lions flashed through my mind. Or even Bigfoot – I'd read stories of sightings over in Burnet, not far from Llano County.

Then a shape formed that resembled a pioneer woman. She wore a long dress and carried an old lantern. I had seen enough. I jumped into my truck and left the park with spinning tires.

I really don't know what I saw. Over the next few trips I subconsciously sped up when I passed the roadside park. I researched on the Internet to see what I could find on this mysterious sighting, but nothing revealed any stories about a woman who walked around with a lantern, or any similar story in this area of Texas.

After about a month, I decided to get brave and try the roadside park again. This time, along with my sandwiches, I packed a 10,000-watt flashlight. As I went through Llano I started to get a little apprehensive but continued on to the park. When I pulled in, I parked so the driver's door was next to the picnic table. No use taking any chances.

Like before, I sat down on top of the picnic table and began to eat. I got there a little earlier then last time and had just started on my second sandwich before it began to get dark. The view of the valley is nice and I enjoy watching the sunset from there.

Everything was quiet in the surrounding brush and hillside, so I stayed a while after finishing my meal. Nothing seemed out of the ordinary so I continued on to my parents' house.

I was a little disappointed, because I actually wanted an occurrence to happen. From then on I stopped at the roadside park on every trip.

After about a month, I stopped at the park to eat a couple of barbeque sandwiches I'd picked up at Cooper's in Llano. I was more into the barbeque than my surrounding.

Suddenly my spine chilled and the hair on my neck stood up, and I knew I was no longer alone. I jerked around, and saw the same woman that I'd seen before watching me. Her hair was in a bun, her dress was ankle length, she held a lantern in one hand and a small quilt in her other hand.

I stammered some unintelligible words and stood up. I backed up a couple of steps and then asked her what she was looking for. She held up the lantern and the quilt and stepped forward closing the distance between us. Suddenly a car came around the bend and its headlights briefly swept over the park, and I could see the trees through the woman. The car swept past and I watched it go down the road. I turned back toward the picnic table and trees, and swept the flashlight over the entire area. The woman had disappeared. I walked a little ways into the brush but didn't find any indications that there had even been anyone in the park with me.

Over the next six months I stopped there periodically but didn't have another sighting. I never found any explanation for this woman's presences. I just figured there might be more to the Baby Head Mountain story than what the historical marker told.

Lately more postings have appeared on the Internet about possible happenings in 1850s, however, the stories do not mention a woman.

After I heard David Tower's story, I also researched stories about Baby Head Mountain and found that Indian raids and sinister plots by the major landowners in the area. There are not any stories related to a woman ghost searching for her baby, as this is what I gathered from the small quilt that she carried. May this young child and her parents rest in peace regardless of how the child died.

It Comes from "The Damp" –
Llano's Six-Mile Light

by Joan Upton Hall

Llano, Texas

Part of growing up in the town of Llano was hearing stories of the Six-Mile Light, but I never took them seriously. Many teenagers made it a rite of passage to go with friends, scaring themselves in quest of the Light at the old cemetery. Even when I was one of those kids and professed to be terrified, I always suspected the only light was a reflection of headlights on the school windows. In fact I was pretty sure that teenagers looking for the legendary orb were the only ones who haunted the place.

I was wrong.

Dale Fry, feature writer for the *Llano Buzz & Country Journal*, who has done extensive investigation, reported in the January 1996 issue of *Enchanted Rock Magazine* that the list of sightings has been long and consistent. These date from the early and mid 1800s. People have described a luminous ball of light that floats here and there and finally disappears leaving no trace. A couple of facts add the chill bumps. It most often appears in the vicinities of the Six-Mile Cemetery and Blount Well, the latter of which has mysterious origins since it was dug before white settlers moved in. Some say the Spanish explorers dug it.

81

A prevalent tale circulating during my school days, related that two young cowboys in the area were riding home about midnight from a dance, when the Light appeared and began to follow them. Unable to get away from the thing, they nearly ran their horses to death until it finally vanished. According to popular tales, "the boys' hair turned white overnight, and they were never the same." According to Fry's article, all except that last part was well documented.

Not long ago I decided to go back and see the location of the Six-Mile Light by day. So my husband Don and I went to the abandoned community of Six-Mile, which is actually about nine miles southwest of Llano on Ranch Road 2323, aka the old Fredericksburg Road. Since the 1990s two Texas medallions have commemorated historical locations near the main road. One tells of the cemetery and an 1883 headstone marking the earliest grave. The other medallion notes the one-room school built next to the cemetery in 1884 and closed in 1945. The building has been renovated and both are well tended now, but that didn't used to be the case.

Local rancher and historian, Mada West, had told Fry that Blount Well, located on her ranch, served as a reliable source for water and was a regular stopping place for travelers who reported the earliest sightings of the Light that she knew of. But an event occurred in 1941 that hit closer to the heart. Her father, Oll Smith, had an encounter of his own. Because tools had been disappearing at a granite quarry, Smith and another man were standing guard one night. West told Dale Fry, "The Six-Mile Light appeared out of nowhere and landed on the handle of a shovel my dad was holding…He spoke to the light and said, 'If you want that shovel you can have it!' and ran." Those two watchmen were the last ones to accept the job of night watchmen at the quarry.

Various reports seemed to indicate that appearances happened on wet, foggy nights, and most sightings were brief. West, however, related that on one occasion in September

1965, people claimed they watched the Light for two hours. They described it as a bright ball that illuminated the area, and it even hovered over Blount Mountain. Other witnesses have described it variously as "bright orange with an iridescent glow," "ghostly," "the size of a wagon wheel," and even "as big as a full moon." Also, while sightings have occurred over a fairly wide area of the county, the location most often pinpointed is around the Six-Mile Cemetery and Blount Well.

Another Llano historian and author, Alline Elliott told Dale Fry that several of her relatives had seen the Light. Most hair-raising of all incidents occurred one night in the 1950s when some local teenagers had gone to the old school house. Sitting in their car at the entrance to the cemetery, they suddenly saw a large ball of light appear and rise from the base of a tree. It moved quickly to the car and hovered in front of the windshield. The kids backed the car away, wheeled around, and raced back to town.

Elliott related another story of the Light and a vehicle. A Llano cafe owner was coming home one night when his car happened to die at the slab over Six-Mile Creek, about two blocks from the cemetery. He was so scared he left the car and ran home.

Fry tells of still another Llano cafe owner, who said that many years ago, her husband saw the Light when he was a young man, working on a ranch at Six-Mile. He was walking home at twilight. "Out of nowhere, a brilliant ball of light streaked across the road in front of him and sped into a pasture, where it suddenly disappeared."

Old-timers spoke of the Light coming up in some instances when somebody dug into wet earth that harbored sulfur deposits. They called such areas "The Damp." Dale Fry cites another article in *Enchanted Rock Magazine*, referring to that terminology, and he quotes Dr. Daniel S. Barker, professor at the University of Texas's School of Economic Geology: "The word 'damp' comes from an old German word, 'dampf,' which means 'gas,' he said. It could be swamp gas, which is methane gas created from matter that has decomposed."

Fry goes on to quote another U.T. professor, Dr. Robert Gutierrez of the Department of Geological Sciences, corroborating Dr. Barker's theory in which he observes, "Gas can be released through a crack in the earth. If it's a graveyard, there's a lot of decomposition."

Swamp gas! Isn't that the same thing authorities have blamed for other unexplained sights – such as UFOs? And if you ask me, UFO descriptions don't sound a whole lot like the descriptions of The Six-Mile Light. As for what might be rising from "The Damp" of the graveyard and Blount Well, something else comes to mind. After all the history of both places goes further back than what is chronicled.

Come to think of it, what decomposition could possibly be left of bodies buried that long ago? Restless spirits, on the other hand – well, that's another matter.

The swamp gas theory raises still another question (as well as the hair on the nape of this writer's neck). Why do these orbs tend to approach folks, hover near them, and even follow them?

Dale Fry's article suggests various other scientific theories for the Six-Mile Light too, but he seems to favor "The Damp" as the culprit. He told me he plans to watch for the phenomenon next wet spell, camera in hand, and whatever he captures on film. I for one want to see it.

The Old Stagecoach Road

by Mitchel Whitington

Marshall, Texas

Marshall, Texas has a wonderful history; in fact, the East Texas city was at one time the Capital of the State of Missouri. The year was 1863, and the last elected officials of the state were fleeing for their lives. Missouri Governor Thomas C. Reynolds found refuge in Texas, and set up the Missouri state government in Marshall, an arrangement that lasted until the end of the Civil War.

Highway 59 bisects the city, and just south of north loop is Poplar Street. If one were to go east and travel four to five miles, the pavement disappears and the road becomes a one-lane path with dirt sides rising eight to ten feet high in some places. At that point, the passage is known as Stagecoach Road.

As the story goes, the old road ran from Marshall to Karnack, and then split to Jefferson, Texas and Shreveport, Louisiana. Originally, it was a Caddo Indian path that had been used for centuries. The stagecoach lines started using the trace in the 1800s, and wore it down over the years to the point where the sides rose above the road. A Texas Historical Marker erected in 1979 to commemorate the road reads as follows:

Marshall-Shreveport Stagecoach Road – Before the Civil War (1861-65), the stage road was the main transportation artery between Marshall and Shreveport, providing a link with

New Orleans for distant markets. Extending northeast from Marshall, the stage road paralleled the later route of State Highway 43 and passed about 2.5 miles north of this site. Merging with the route from Jefferson, it turned southeast toward Waskom. In some areas, iron-rimmed wheels and horses' hooves trampled the narrow roadbed as much as 12 feet below the surrounding terrain. Travel over the dirt road was uncomfortable in dry weather and often impossible in rainy seasons. Regular stage service was established by 1850, with three arrivals and three departures weekly from Marshall. Arrival of the stage was a major event. At the sound of the driver's bugle, townspeople rushed to meet the incoming coach. By 1860 Marshall had several stagecoach lines and a network of roads. The Marshall to Shreveport line was operated by plantation owner William Bradfield and his son John. The stage continued to run during the Civil War, despite the shortage of drivers and horses. Use of the stage road declined after the war, when the Southern Pacific completed a rail line to Shreveport.

Because the stagecoach had to travel through the countryside, there were always delays when bridges were flooded out or creeks rose. Eventually the railroad became a more practical mode of travel and shipping, and the old Stagecoach Road was used only by the people who lived in that area.

Today, the road has been preserved, and is now a popular path for horseback riders and hikers. To celebrate its history, the city of Marshall holds an annual "Stagecoach Days" celebration, which is the third weekend in May. It features arts and crafts, food booths, a transportation parade, horseshoe tournament, a potluck cook-off, and performances by local musicians (more information is available from the Chamber of Commerce: 903-935-7868). Website?

As one might expect from a road that his been used as far back as history has been recorded, there are many associated ghost stories. Local legend tells of a funeral procession that travels the road, and also the sounds of galloping horses pulling a stage that pass in the night. Most people dismiss such tales as fanciful imagination and folklore.

There are some local residents, however, who tell a more sinister side to the history of Stagecoach Road. More than one person has related the story of an indigent work farm located on the road in the early 1900s, which was basically a minimum-security prison for those convicted of debt-related crimes.

The guards were supposedly hard taskmasters, because the fields that the prisoners worked were the property of the warden who sold the resulting crops.

The workers that could not produce were supposedly whipped and beaten, and those who did not survive were buried in a pauper's cemetery along Stagecoach Road.

Even darker legends say that after the Civil War, the freed slaves who joined the Carpetbaggers from the north who led the Reconstruction of the southern states were hanged from the trees that still overshadow the road, and their bodies left swinging there as a warning to others.

Today, along with the previously mentioned apparitions, ghost light activity has been reported along the old, dirt road. Some have snapped photos showing these lights, but many have witnessed them with the naked eye.

Whether any of this is true is a topic that is perpetually under debate. Most view Stagecoach Road in Marshall as a landmark to a bygone era, although there are some that say it has a decidedly supernatural side when the sun goes down, and the road is dark and lonely.

Whatever the case, Stagecoach Road is a fascinating throwback to another era that has somehow escaped the pitfalls of progress.

Hairy Man Road
by Joy Nord

Round Rock, Texas

Occasionally on Sunday afternoons, before Richard and I were married, we mounted his steel horse (a motorcycle) and rode around the countryside. One of his favorite roads to cruise was Hairy Man Road. He didn't think it was scary but I did. While riding along this curving road, I always wrapped my arms around him a little tighter, and rested my face on his back because I was scared.

Hairy Man Road starts in Round Rock off of Sam Bass Road and ends at U.S. Highway 183 in Cedar Park. Before the road improvements a few years back, tree branches, from both sides of the road, formed a canopy that covered the narrow, winding eight-mile span. Fortunately, the area of Hairy Man Road in Round Rock where the hairy man legend was drawn still has its significant charm: stately tall trees and fern bluffs that run along Brushy Creek. Today Hairy Man Road is also known as Brushy Creek Road and, also, County Road 174, which complicates directions.

Legend claims that on a dark stormy night in the mid-1800s, a young boy became separated from his parents when a caravan of settlers tried to escape the rising waters of the nearby creek. The boy managed to survive on his own. However, the separation from his family and the near death experience from drowning traumatized him, and he became a hermit. He avoided communication with people and terrorized those who threatened his domain – the thick undergrowth and trees along Brushy Creek.

He would jump out from the trees and frighten stagecoach drivers and horses, solitary riders, and anyone who dared to trespass near his neck of the woods. He also climbed the trees and dragged his feet across the top of passing carriages. Then one day, when he tried to intimidate another victim, a team of galloping horses trampled him to death. On that day, a hairy man's death may have given birth to a legend. To this day, many people swear that they have seen a large hairy man lurking alongside the road and within the woods of the hiking trails. Teenagers, or should I say "the male gender," use the road for thrill seeking, and with the hopes of scaring their dates into the safety of their arms.

Through the years, several versions of the hairy man's story have been passed down from generation to generation. One such tale claims that he raised goats and after a while hair started to grow all over his body like the creatures he cared for. Thereafter, the hairy man became known as Goat Man. And he even developed horns. Could the hairy man actually have been Harry Mann, a goat farmer who lived near the road along the creek?

However the Williamson County records do not indicate anyone by that name has ever lived in the county during the legend's time period.

Since 1994 the Brushy Creek Women's Association and the Brushy Creek MUD have sponsored the Hairy Man Festival held in October. This family fun-filled event raises money for many local charities and offers a day of food, arts and crafts, children's activities, special performances, live music, and a hairiest man contest.

Historians, and long-time landowners along the creek, are baffled by who or what the hairy man was. No one knows for sure. Whether the tales are truth or fiction, the Hairy Man remains alive through storytellers such as Gwen King who continues to tell his tale at the Hairy Man Festival.

The Ghost of Jake

by Bettey Baldwin

Hutto, Texas

Can a rural ghost survive in a suburban world?

It seems the ghost of Jake's Hill Road will have to learn how to deal with a busy, modern world or move on to the next plane of existence.

There was a time when searching for the ghost of Jake's Hill Road was a dark and spooky event along the narrow, winding road led from Hutto to Pflugerville. Whether by the full moon or new moon it was a shadowy, dark drive ending next to a cemetery.

The bridge was made even darker by the large trees growing along the banks of Brushy Creek. It was said the best spot to find Jake's ghost was on the old bridge crossing Brushy Creek. That bridge is no longer there and even its replacement is no longer in use.

There are several stories about who Jake was and why he came to haunt the area.

The oldest story is that Jake was a Blackland Prairie cotton farmer early in the twentieth century. This was a hard way to make a living in the best of times, but for several years in the late 1920s cotton prices were good and Jake did well by his family. In 1929 the price of cotton was the highest it had ever been and everyone was prosperous. People expanded their

91

farms and businesses. In order to expand they went in debt to the bank.

Then on Black Tuesday in late October stock prices started falling. The market lost a significant portion of its value in one day. The crash didn't stop there. The market kept falling until it was half of what it had been. Money was no longer easily come by.

Prices fell, but even with low prices there still wasn't enough money to keep cotton prices up to a point where Jake could make the payments on his farm. Trying to make the payments agreed upon when money was readily available became an impossible task, not just for Jake, but for all farmers. Within a couple of years the price of cotton was so low farmers couldn't even feed their families much less make their payments on their farms.

Without their land, farmers couldn't support their families. This downward spiral led to many tragedies. Jake was one of them.

Being refused after trying to talk the bank into extending his credit, he went home and shot his wife and their two children. Then he went to the bridge that crossed Brushy Creek and hanged himself from it. One variation I've heard is that the reason he chose that bridge is because the banker who was foreclosing on the farm had to drive over it to get home from the bank.

Some people claim to have spotted two ghostly children in the area as well. These could be Jake's children, but since I didn't hear about these ghosts until after two other children were killed and their bodies hidden near the bridge in the nineties, it might be there are some new ghosts in the vicinity.

Another story says Jake was actually a young man who murdered his parents and drove their car with the bodies in it off the bridge. He then died in a house fire.

Before the road was reworked a couple of years ago, when driving in the area at night (something I got to do a lot of when taking kids home from events at the school) the headlights would pick out one particular tombstone in the cemetery. I went to look at it during the day once and have to report it did not belong to anyone who might be called Jake.

The area is still spooky at night, but not totally dark. The other night when I drove past the area light pollution from surrounding communities bounced off clouds creating an eerie mango-colored haze. This strange light reflecting off clouds almost makes the area scarier than when it is pitch-dark.

It is still a favorite spot among the high school crowd. Boys like to take their girlfriends out there and enjoy the benefits of calming their fears about any ghostly apparitions that might appear. Since the roadwork was completed there is only a dead end lane leading to the cemetery. It goes just a bit past, and stops short of Brushy Creek, so now it is less dangerous to park out there; at least as far as traffic is concerned.

Nowadays, adding to the fright value, you can sometimes hear dogs howling nearby. That could be pretty scary if you didn't realize you were close to Triple Crown Academy, one of the premier dog training and dog hotel facilities in the United States. It does add to the overall, eerie effect of the place though. Just think about it, a graveyard, an abandoned bridge where a man supposedly hanged himself, dogs howling and baying, and bodies dumped nearby all makes for a really scary spot. Then, when you get a night fog drifting around the overall feel is as unnerving as Conan Doyle's *The Hound of the Baskerville*.

Austin Ghosts Along Congress Avenue

by Robert Fears

Austin is a beautiful city located in central Texas. It is built upon rolling to steep topography of the Hill Country with clear, cool creeks meandering through the city and emptying into the Colorado River. A great diversity of people live and work in Austin including university students, politicians, musicians, actors/actresses, computer technicians, and cowboys. Austin is the state capital, a business and cultural center, and is surrounded by ranches and farms. But Austin is also reported to have a dark side.

The city's slogan, "Keep Austin Weird," is displayed on bumper stickers, t-shirts, billboards, and various other promotional materials. This slogan was adopted by the Austin Independent Business Alliance to promote small businesses. It is felt by many citizens that a multitude of small businesses in Austin give the city its unique cultural identity. Many believe that an increase of major corporations would make Austin normal.

Webster defines weird as eerie, ghostly, strange, supernatural, uncanny, unearthly, and witching. Due to all of the recorded ghost sightings, Webster's definition of weird probably fits Austin better than that used by the business alliance.

A downtown center of activity in Austin is Congress Avenue that runs downhill from the front steps of the Capital and across the Colorado River. This area features fine restaurants, first class hotels, retail stores, offices, theaters, and nightclubs. One of the recreational opportunities is walking tours conducted by companies who deal in ghosts.

Eerie undertones of this downtown area are thought by some to initiate from an estimated 750,000 bats that roost under the Congress Avenue Bridge each spring and summer. A scientific reason for this event is that narrow and deep openings under the bridge deck provide good habitat for these flying mammals. Mythically, bats can be transformed vampires or a symbol of ghosts or death. Some American Indian tribes believed that bats are trickster spirits who disobey normal rules and norms of behavior. Around sunset bats emerge like a big, black cloud from underneath the Congress Avenue Bridge in search of food. On some evenings, shortly after the bats take flight, people along Congress Avenue begin to report encounters with ghosts from Austin's past.

The southeast corner of Congress Avenue and Third Street, also called the House District, was the seat of Austin's most gruesome history. This is the prior site of the Pearl House, a small railroad hotel that was later acknowledged as a house of ill repute. It is theorized that Jack the Ripper operated from this hotel during 1884 and 1885 before moving to London to continue his hideous crimes. During his killing spree in Austin as many as twenty people, mostly women, who were attacked and at least seven of them were brutally killed. Most attacks occurred within a few blocks of the Pearl House.

Pearl House employed a Malay cook who moved to London soon after the Austin murders ceased. Similar killings began in London soon after his arrival. Although he was never caught, he still remains the primary suspect. Empty lots and pavement now mark the Austin murder sites. No one wants to build on these sites even though they are prime commercial real estate. It is said that people unconsciously cross the street rather than walk by these areas to avoid powerful and ugly energy radiating from them.

At 412 Congress Avenue is Speakeasy, a signature nightclub fashioned after the secret clubs of prohibition. Speakeasy is in the historic Kreisel Building that completely burned on July 26, 1916. Two women, who became trapped in an elevator, and a fireman were killed in the fire. This same, now antique, elevator is suspended above the main stage where people claim they have seen a woman's apparition. Some have heard the front doors bang followed by a sound of someone running up and down the 59-step stair case to the roof terrace. Then there is a knocking on the walls followed by a scream. Sometimes only screams are heard.

On the corner of Congress Avenue and Sixth Street is the Littlefield Building, a financial center built on the site of the old Iron Front Saloon. The Iron Front Saloon was owned and operated by a gunslinger named, Ben Thompson. While owning the saloon, Thompson ran for city marshal and won after shooting his opponent. He actually made a good marshal and established law and order in Austin. In March 1884, while in San Antonio, he was ambushed and killed. Upon examination of his body, nine bullets were found in his back. Thompson's footsteps are still heard in the Littlefield Building and his cigar smoke is smelled in this smoke-free building. People say that his ghost is responsible for empty elevators that operate themselves.

Major George Washington Littlefield, owner and builder of the building, is also said to haunt the premises. He is sometimes heard clearing his throat in the lobby and on the top floor. His outline or even a brief glimpse of his face has been seen at the top floor, third window from the left, on the Sixth Street side of the building.

In this same vicinity is The Hideout, a recently renovated theater. This building had been vacant during most of the nineties and was owned by a Houston family since before Texas was a state. It has been a saloon, a dry cleaning shop, a men's clothing store and a pawnshop. It appears that some people who conducted business in the building have never left. Faucets turn on and off and locked gates open. During recent renovation, the main breaker was tripped for no apparent reason.

The Paramount Theater is located in the block just north of The Hideout and is another old building where spirits are said to thrive. This theater was built in 1915 at a cost of $150,000. The primary ghost in this building seems to be that of Walter Norris, a longtime, much beloved projectionist who died while showing *Casablanca* in 2000. Ken Stein, Paramount's Executive Director, says that sometimes projection equipment will not work unless someone puts chocolate doughnuts or Snickers bars in the booth. Those were Walter Norris' favorite snacks. Whispers have also been heard from the projection room when no one is there. The custodian at the Paramount says that he had an eerie experience in the auditorium when he heard footsteps behind him. When he looked around, no one was there. He said that two weeks later he was in the same spot and he heard somebody get out of a seat right behind him.

At least two ghosts are known to haunt the Capital building. One reported ghost is that of former governor Edmund Jackson Davis, who ran for reelection in December of 1873 and was defeated. Davis declared the election illegal and refused to leave the Capital taking control of the lower floor and surrounding himself with state police. The new governor was forced to occupy the second floor. Davis appealed to President Ulysses S. Grant for military support and was denied. It was then that Davis was removed from office and forced to resign.

It is said that Governor Davis still haunts his old offices, looking sadly out of a window or gazing off into space as if he is confused. Others hear footsteps and odd rattling noises on the first floor. Davis has also been reported walking on the Capital grounds on misty days. He has been described as a tall man with a full beard, flowing mustache and an icy glare. It is said, at times he will stand completely still and let people pass before resuming his walk. At other times, they say he appears lost in thought and seems to be pacing.

A second ghost of the Capital is that of Robert Marshall Love, a prior State Comptroller. In June of 1903, Love was fatally shot at his desk by W.G. Hill, a former employee. Love's image has been captured by many of the security cameras that surround the Capital. He is frequently seen by visitors walking through walls on the second floor.

Congress Avenue offers only a small sample of Austin ghosts. Austin has been said to have more ghosts per block than any city in America. Ghosts have been reported in the Governor's Mansion, St. Edwards University, The University of Texas, Driskill Hotel, old cemeteries, beds and breakfasts, and many other restaurants and clubs. However, the easiest way to spend an eerie evening in Austin is to begin at Congress Avenue Bridge to view the bats at sunset and then stroll along the avenue visiting places reported to be haunted. You may or may not see ghosts but it is almost guaranteed that someone will tell you a ghost story.

The Ghost Road Light

by Mitchel Whitington

Saratoga, Texas

Just stop for a moment and imagine that it is a dark, moonless night in Hardin County. You're driving along the backroads, and turn onto Farm-to-Market Road 787 – or FM 787 as it is known locally – and something very strange occurs. At the end of the road ahead of you there is a soft glow, a hovering light that seems to be taunting you, weaving about as if it is studying you as much as you are watching it.

What is this strange phenomenon? The Ghost Road light, of course, a regular occurrence in Hardin County. It's been called the Bragg Road Light, the Hardin County Light, the Ghost Road Light, and many other names on television shows and in printed media. What the light might actually be has been the subject of much debate over the years, and to be honest, to this day no one knows for sure. It has been well documented in photographs, and studied by many reputable sources such as *National Geographic*. With all of the stories surrounding it, there is one fact that cannot be disputed: the light exists.

The road itself has its origin back in the logging days of East Texas, long before the timber giants of today established controlled cutting and re-planting procedures. The entire area was known as the Big Thicket because of its wealth and population of native trees, with dense, impassible underbrush. To this day it is said to be one of the most biologically diverse places around. A large number of bird species stopped there on annual treks, and wildlife inhabiting the Thicket included wild rabbit, deer, wolves, panthers, bears and too many others to list here. They made their home among the trees, and humans who wandered in had to be exceptionally careful to find their way back out. With a simple turn in the wrong direction, one tree would start looking like the next. When you were in the Big Thicket, there were no defining landmarks to guide your way. The darkness of the forest would simply close in on you.

Anticipating the wealth of raw resources there, the Gulf, Colorado and Santa Fe Railway (GCSF) bought a nine-mile right-of-way through the land in 1902. They saw an unlimited potential of hauling lumber out of the thicket off to mills, moving oil as wells spread across Texas, and also hoped to capitalize on the additional revenue from carrying livestock to market. Of course, any passenger trade would be icing on the financial cake. The railroad started at their main line at the small town of Bragg, which had been named for Confederate General Braxton Bragg, and chopped their way south through the forest to the town of Saratoga. The last bit was cleared in January of 1904, and the GCSF begin laying timbers and tracks for the railroad spur.

Rumors of hauntings along the railway line begin circulating almost immediately. One story attributed the ghost to a Union sympathizer during the Civil War. During that time, the Thicket was a natural place for criminals and such to hide out, and Confederate troops would set fire to the forest to flush out the unsavory characters there. As the legend goes, the troops were doing a routine burning when they saw a known Yankee sympathizer running from the flames. Several soldiers opened fire, killing the man, then leaving his body to be consumed by the fire and the forest. His ghost was said to walk through the forest in the form of a glowing light, walking the escape path that he'd taken that fateful day.

Other people claimed that the spirits went further back in time, when Spanish soldiers occupied the area. In their quest for treasure and the legendary "Seven Cities of Gold" the Spaniards actually found very little wealth. What they did find, this story tells, they hid in the Thicket to return and retrieve later. The plan of those scheming conquistadors was discovered, and although the men were executed as traitors, searchers could not find the treasure that they'd hidden in the forest. The mysterious light was supposedly one of those slain solders, vigilantly guarding their treasure even after his death.

One more explanation for the ghostly light seen along the railroad line was that it was the spirit of a hunter who had ventured into the Big Thicket in search of game, even though he wasn't familiar with the terrain there. After a successful day of shooting small game, he headed back toward home, but had become hopelessly lost in the dense forest growth. Because of the abundance of animals and edible plants, he is said to have survived for quite some time before falling prey to one of the perils of the Thicket. In this version of the story, the light is the ghost of the hunter, still wandering the forest in search of a way home.

These stories were all circulating at the time when the GCSF Railway was still in operation, so reports of the mysterious light easily date back to the early 1900s.

After thirty years of operation, the Saratoga Branch ceased to be profitable. Mr. Cowley, the GCSF Gulf Division Superintendent, is quoted as saying, "The Gulf, Colorado and Santa Fe Railway enjoyed a good business out of Saratoga after the construction of the line for several years, but it dwindled away due to the construction of pipelines for the handling of the oil and to the diminution of the lumber traffic. There were several mills on the line, one principal one operated by the McShane Lumber Company, which cut out in 1915. Subsequently, traffic into and out of Saratoga dwindled down to merchandise, flour and feed and gasoline, and outbound logs or stave blocks or staves, but each year the traffic of the branch decreased." In 1933, the railroad spur was abandoned.

Hardin County purchased the right-of-way from the GCSF in 1934 with the idea that it would make a good county road out to Saratoga, and its road crews set about the process of pulling up the rails and digging up the timbers. The road was built, and the sightings of the ghostly light continued.

Throughout the years, the topic of harvesting lumber from the Big Thicket has been broached by several corporations, so to try and preserve the beautiful forest the Big Thicket Association was formed. In 1995, the Association commissioned a study of the bio/ecology of the area around Bragg Road (as the county highway had come to be known). Several different ecosystems were discovered to exist there, including Baygall, Prairie, Palmetto Flat, and Wetland Savannah. According to this study, over forty different types of trees and shrubs were identified, over thirty types of flowering plants, and other vegetative species such as ferns and vines. Armed with this information, a fight to preserve the area around Bragg Road was launched and on July 28, 1997 the Hardin County Commissioners Court voted to designate the area as the "Ghost Road Scenic Drive County Park," insuring that it would be protected in the future.

The current story that a visitor is likely to hear today concerns a brakeman who was killed in a tragic train wreck. There are several versions of the story circulating around, but the more interesting ones have the poor man getting decapitated in the accident – of course, they only found his body. The brakeman apparently still walks the path of the tracks, looking for his missing head. An addendum to the story goes that a decade after the wreck, another train was rolling down the track on a moonless, stormy evening when they saw a light swinging back and forth on the tracks ahead. The engineer slowed the locomotive, and as it came to a stop the crew saw that a huge tree trunk had been blown over the tracks. It would have spelled disaster had the train hit it at full speed, probably causing a derailment and disaster to everyone on board. When the train crew jumped down to try to move the tree trunk, they began searching for the man whose light had saved their lives, he was no where to be found – they decided that it was the spirit of the brakeman who'd helped them advert danger that night.

As rousing a story as the beheaded brakeman makes, it is probably not an accurate account of what is happening out on Bragg Road. There aren't any credible accounts of train wrecks on the nine-mile spur during its thirty years of operation, and the fact that the light was appearing even as the railroad was being constructed indicates that the mysterious glowing objects pre-dates the first train through that part of Big Thicket.

Skeptics like to write off the light to some kind of luminous "swamp gas," while others say that it is only the reflection of car headlights. Of course, headlights certainly don't translate well to when the light was first reported so many years ago. Still, everyone has an explanation or opinion. The one thing that no one can dispute is that the light is there – just ask *National Geographic*, because even though they can't explain it, they saw that it was undeniably there.

Old Stone Ridge Road and the Donkey Lady Legends

by Carol MacDonald Menchu

Austin & San Antonio, Texas

There are two "Old" Stone Ridge Roads within 250 miles of each other: one in Austin and one in San Antonio. Both are actually named Stone Ridge Road, without the "old," and each have reference to a "Donkey Lady" haunting the area.

Stone Ridge Road in Austin winds around South Austin off the South Capital of Texas Highway. There is an old cemetery on that road – the Tucker Cemetery.

As the legend goes, there is a children's cemetery in the area devoted to stillborns, infants, and toddlers. The belief is that a horribly disfigured Donkey Lady appears on the road to protect the children from harm. It is said that the Donkey Lady was mangled and killed in an automobile wreck not far from the cemetery. Today, she reportedly puts dents in cars and breaks windshields. Sightings of orbs and floating objects have also been documented.

There is, however, nothing to back up the story that the graveyard is a "children's cemetery." It is actually named Tucker Cemetery and was created by Martha Susan Teague Tucker when she buried her husband, Ellis Henry Tucker in January, 1880.

Stone Ridge Road in San Antonio is in the Hollywood Park area near Oakhaven Park, and while stories of the Donkey Lady abound in San Antonio, none of them take place near this particular Stone Ridge Road, nor is it mentioned in any of the legends.

The first legend comes from the Helotes area, northwest of San Antonio on State Highway 16. Allegedly the Donkey Lady haunts the woods outside of town and has been seen there. A search of 'hauntings' in the Helotes area reveals three unidentified female ghosts seen in wooded areas, none of which fit the description of the supposedly burned and mutilated Donkey Lady.

The second legend comes from the Windcrest area of San Antonio, just southeast of the intersection of Interstate-410 and Interstate-35 and north of Walzem Road.

These stories tell us of a woman named Doc Anderson who became known as the Donkey Lady of Live Oak because she kept rare donkeys, and the Skunk Lady of Windcrest because she could live with wild skunks under her house without being sprayed by the animals.

After coming on hard times, the Donkey Lady and her partner, who was either her husband or her brother, ended up living in a tin and cardboard shack with no running water or electricity. For years, people in the neighborhood helped by carrying water to her shack.

Those who knew Doc Anderson said she was a sad person of pale complexion with long hair and her clothes, those of a bag-lady. One story says she had only one arm. She was often seen at night, walking her donkeys along Weidner Road. After 1982, Doc Anderson dropped out of sight, but those who knew her say she died in the 1990s.

The truth of Doc Anderson, the Donkey Lady, became legend, and in doing so, grew into the third legend.

The Donkey Lady in legend three is a recluse who was horribly burned – her fingers fused together, becoming like

105

hooves. This story is that her husband set their house on fire burning her to the point of being horribly mutilated and also killing her children, leaving her insane.

Or is she the lady who raised and kept donkeys in this area? This story has one of her donkeys biting a child whose father, in anger, ambushed her on a bridge causing both her and the donkey to fall into the water and drown.

This bridge plays heavily on all the manifestations of the Donkey Lady of legend number three. Located somewhere on either Applewhite Road or Zarzamora Road, it became a popular hangout for teens, especially on Halloween.

She has been said to terrorize people, mostly teenagers, who come to the bridge at night. She appears, braying like a donkey and throwing herself at the vehicles to cause dents, scratches, and broken windshields. The descriptions for her in this incarnation are those of the burned, disfigured lady with hooves for hands – the Donkey Lady.

One of the wilder urban legends about the Donkey Lady supposedly specifies a telephone number that one could call to hear her bray.

Is the Donkey Lady of South San Antonio an incarnation of Doc Anderson, the Donkey Lady of North San Antonio?

To add to the confusion, there is a cemetery in the area of Stone Ridge Road in San Antonio. Where and when did the San Antonio Stone Ridge Road Donkey Lady legend begin and why is it not in the memories of San Antonio, only those of Austin?

Does this mean then, that the haunting on "Old" Stone Ridge Road in Austin is a melding of memory of the San Antonio story and a real haunting in Austin now lost in the legend of the Donkey Lady?

Austin's Stone Ridge Road is South on MoPac Expressway to Capital of Texas Highway (State Loop 360) just beyond the Barton Creek Square Shopping Center, right on Capital of Texas Highway to Stone Ridge Road. Right on

Stone Ridge which winds around back toward and crossing Walsh Tarlton Lane, ending at Thousand Oaks Drive.

San Antonio's Stone Ridge Road is in North San Antonio in Hollywood Park, east of U.S. Highway 281 and south of State Loop 1604, to the north of Thousand Oaks Drive.

The Haunting of Post Nine

by Joy Nord

Camp Swift, Texas

The full moon bathed the land in a waxy glow. Puffy clouds drifted through an indigo sky dotted with stars, and light rippled off the swollen waters of a nearby creek.

Somewhere within the piney woods an owl hooted, a solitary voice in the night.

Two Metro Care employees waited at the corner of State Highway 95 and Ranch Road 2236. Their parked location, known as Post Nine, is an EMS vehicle standby station, a place where waiting makes the difference between life and death along the desolate roads of Bastrop County.

While the engine's hum lulled Clayton to sleep, Marris remained wide awake and listened. Not necessarily for an emergency dispatch, because her partner would suddenly become alert to that, but for the sound of scraping tree branches on the truck and the cry from an unknown source. The truck sat on a heap of rocks and barren soil twenty-five feet from the tree line where at times medics have heard an eerie sound – but oddly enough, only the female medics.

Marris recalled the first time she heard the noises. With flashlight in hand she walked around the truck, checked underneath, and even hoisted herself to look on top.

During her investigation the scraping noise stopped and she didn't see anything that was touching the truck; however when she got back into the cab the sounds resumed.

Being leery of the unknown had never bothered Marris until she was told the history of Camp Swift and the murder of an eight-year-old girl in 1942. For Marris, the unsettling events of the past and circumstances of the present were creepy.

Camp Swift, bordered by State Highway 95 and U.S. Highway 290, twenty-eight miles east of Austin, was built in 1942 on 55,906 acres of hilly uplands and flat lowlands.

Within 120 days nearly three hundred buildings were constructed to accommodate 44,000 troops. The camp was named after Texas native Major General Eden Swift who fought in the Indian Wars of 1876 and during World War I commanded Allied forces in Italy.

Initially Camp Swift was an Infantry training facility that reached a maximum strength of 90,000 troops. During World War II it became the largest army training and transshipment camp in Texas. As one of the twenty-four prisoner of war camps within the state, it housed 3,865 German soldiers and some 300 Russians who had been forced to fight on the German side, but had to be segregated from the Germans in the camp.

After the war, the camp was decommissioned in 1946 and much of the site was returned to former owners. It included a POW cemetery where at least eleven German soldiers remain buried. Three other cemeteries exist with a fence protecting two of them.

The third, a pioneer cemetery, consists of three graves, a father and his two sons who were killed by Indians.

During World War II, Camp Swift had more impact on Bastrop County than any occurrence, by nature or man, before or since. Almost overnight, 5,000 soldiers and civilian employees moved into Camp Swift and the town of Bastrop changed dramatically from a small town of 1,000 inhabitants to a metropolis of more than 50,000 people.

Unfortunately, as the population increased, so did crime.

On weekends, when passes were issued, as many as 25,000 soldiers would be transported to Bastrop on flatbed trucks where they could remain in town or be bussed to Austin. Residents frequently invited soldiers into their homes for Sunday dinners: such was the tradition for County Judge C. B. Maynard, who was also a Major in the Judge Advocate General's Office at Camp Swift. However, his generosity ended the week of October 6, 1942.

On Tuesday afternoon the Judge's eight-year-old daughter, Lucy, failed to return home from school. Since the school was located only two blocks from her home, an immediate search was issued by city officials and the military police at Camp Swift were notified of the missing child. All personnel of the camp took part in a thorough search of the camp area, and that night, officers and men stood by ready to render any assistance possible.

Meanwhile in Austin a man gassed up a Lincoln Zephyr at the Gulf Station on the corner of Duval and 29th Street, and drove off without paying. The gas station attendee reported to the Austin police the license plate number and that the thief wore a military uniform. Consequently the police alerted Camp Swift officials. Several hours later, the Austin police picked up Pvt. George Knapp, 38, of St. Paul, Minnesota, who was driving a stolen car, reported missing earlier that day from Lt. George Noonan. Although confined, Knapp slept in the comforts of a warm cell while little Lucy Maynard lay unconscious and exposed to the night's chill with a crushed larynx.

The following afternoon, after a twenty-two hour search, Lucy was found unconscious, and in a convulsive state, in a ravine several miles north of Bastrop on Highway 95 toward Camp Swift. She was rushed to the Orgain Memorial Hospital where she died early the next morning from pneumonia brought on by exposure.

Knapp was turned over to military authorities at 12:30 a.m. on Thursday. After being questioned about the missing girl, he admitted that he saw her walking home from school and offered her a ride. Finally he expanded on the details. While he drove around Bastrop, the girl became scared and started to scream, he strangled her with his hands and then threw her into the pasture where she was later found. Knapp's confession led to an immediate court marshal, and conviction of the murder of Lucy Rivers Maynard, and he was sentenced to hang.

On the day of Lucy Maynard's funeral, another development in the fast moving case shocked the entire community and beyond. The United Press dispatch from Stillwater, Minnesota, stated that Knapp had been an inmate of a Minnesota hospital for the insane from February 18, 1931 to May 31, 1933. He had been released on the latter date as cured. Camp Swift officials also admitted that Knapp was a draftee with a criminal record.

Five months after the tragedy, Knapp was taken from the stockade at Fort Sam Houston to Leon Springs Military Reservation, twenty miles NW of San Antonio. On the morning of March 19, 1943, a lone member of the Maynard family stood and watched from a platform seventy-five feet away to another platform where gallows that had been constructed. As George Knapp climbed the traditional thirteen steps he spoke with his guards. When he reached the top of the platform he looked in the direction of the witnesses and said, "Say, folks, I didn't rape that little girl – I want you to know that."

During a light rain, Knapp dropped to his death.

Marris shivered in the ambulance. She was in the business of saving people's lives, not remembering how they died. However the memory of *ToriKorosu,* which means *Haunted to Death* in Japanese, entered her mind. Not knowing the details of the Lucy Maynard story, a few months earlier, Marris had allowed her eight-year-old daughter, Meara, to star in a five-minute film produced by Wild Imagination Films that can be seen on YouTube. Meara played the role of a little girl ghost who haunted an ambulance and tries to kill the patients either by inflicting a deep neck injury or by strangulation.

Although Meara and Lucy never killed anyone, what tends to be "creepy" is their resemblance. The girls, both with fair skin, blue eyes, and flaxen hair, look so much alike they could be sisters. Or the same child reincarnated.

Although little Lucy's body physically died in the hospital, one has to wonder does her earth bound spirit still seek help from female medics parked at Post Nine? Or maybe it is the spirit of a German POW or a pioneer that taunts the female emergency personal who are stationed at Post Nine.

The Thompson Island Bridge Ghost

by Barbara Landry

San Marcos, Texas

Certain places lend themselves more to ghostly phenomenon than others. Places, for instance, where great physical pain and distress occurred. Others where the soul was greatly troubled, or their lives seemed to be suddenly and unjustly cut short. And so, they linger.

Such is the case in the area of the Thompson Island Bridge that runs across the San Marcos River off Cape Road between Interstate 35 and State Highway 123. The island is formed because it lies between the raceway from Cape's Dam and the main stem of the San Marcos River. Actually, there are two islands that form as the raceway forks and the right fork flows back into the river upstream of Cape's Road.

The bridge was named for William A. Thompson, a plantation owner from Louisiana who settled in this area in 1850. However the ghost sightings have nothing to do with Thompson, rather that of a Confederate soldier. The first reports of this wandering spirit date as far back as the 1920s.

The story has it that there were two brothers that lived in the area and volunteered to fight with the Confederate Army. Both vowed to return when the war was over, but only one brother, in fact, came home. The other is said to stand guard today at the old Thompson Island Bridge, seen at times by some, but not others.

This is how one witness experienced the sighting. In 1939, Dr. Roy A. Pennycuick and a fellow employee were returning from a trip to South Texas. They were carrying with them $25,000 in collected GMAC funds, and their destination was a police station in San Marcos where the money could be locked in a safe for the night. The hour was late and both men decided to take a short cut on the last few miles of a very long road trip. A fine mist hovered over the narrow road and the river nearby. The tall pecan and cypress trees cast shadows into the crisp autumn air. Suddenly, a loud pop sounded and the car swerved.

Roy held tight to the steering wheel and brought the car to a safe slow stop. A tire had gone flat. There was nothing to do but get it changed, and get it changed fast. Roy was working as swiftly as he could when he began to sense a presence, as if someone was close by. About ten paces from him, a man stood watching them. He was tall and shirtless. His pants were butternut homespun tucked down in infantry boots. He wore a Confederate flat cap and leaned on a muzzle-loading rifle. He didn't speak or move; the man just stood there watching them with a slight grin. What was actually about ten minutes seemed more like an eternity. Then as suddenly as he had appeared, the strange man was gone.

There was nothing leaving any evidence of this spiritual encounter but the stunned expressions on the faces of Roy and a fellow employee.

Several years later Roy had his sighting of the transparent apparition of the Confederate soldier affirmed. While meeting with friends in San Antonio, he met with Lt. Colonel Scott Townsend who had served as provost marshal at Camp Swift, near Bastrop during World War II. The Lt. Colonel knew of the apparition that had been seen on numerous occasions at the Thompson Island Bridge. Townsend, himself, had gone to the location and encountered the spirit of the Confederate soldier after receiving many accounts by Camp Swift soldiers that had crossed the bridge at night. The reports of these encounters were a subject of many conversations and were valid enough to be recorded.

Time has passed and there have been no accounts of recent sightings of the Confederate soldier. Has his mission of guarding the bridge been completed and has his spirit found peace and completely passed over to the other side? Maybe he finally heard the words, "mission accomplished; the war is over, you made it home."

The Imprint
by Julia Byrd

San Marcos, Texas

Within the hills of the Texas Hill Country, a place of darkness and despair is tucked away just a hair's width from the modern world. Discovering this place seemed only a coincidence on a dark summer night, as my friends and I drove around the back roads in my brother's classic, a 1972 Monte Carlo. On that particular careless night, we cruised with the windows down feeling carefree. I turned into the Eagles Peak subdivision off of Ranch Road 12, west of San Marcos, with the intent on finding the "A" hill. It was a spot known to a few locals as the past haunt of Indians, a great location for a sunset view and an evening time scare. Instead, what we found was a place that exceeded our expectations.

As I drove into the subdivision, an urge came over me to turn right at the end of a street onto a cul-de-sac that sits at the top of a small hill. Locals claim the site is quiet most nights. However as I put the car in park, the scene of a terrible deed unfolded before my eyes.

It felt like being in a dream, unable to wake up. As I turned to look at my passenger, I felt something overtake my body. As the feeling begin to overwhelm me, I saw a woman beside me, dressed in 70s-era clothing looking at me with romantic intent. Barely holding onto my senses, the scene took a turn for the worst as the make-out session turned into a sexual assault.

116

Every feeling was clear and vivid to me, and my body shuddered with the energy of sadness, despair and anger. The scene ended as quickly and unexpected as it begun, with the question "Why me?" lingering in the air. As a veteran of paranormal encounters, I could feel that whomever the victim had been of this terrible deed had lived, and as she made her way through life, this question always returned to haunt her. Coupled with the residual feelings of that incident, and the fear of something else happening, I put the car in reverse and lit out of there as quickly as I could. I did not want to see that again.

A few months later, I returned filled with fear and curiosity. Those who had been with me that night when I had my experience had become excited over the prospect of another scare.

We were not disappointed.

As we sat in the car, listening to the sounds of the night, the air bristled with an unearthly presence that seemed to draw closer to the car. All of us could feel it. Still and waiting, our breath began to shorten. I could hear the rising sounds of war drums. Turning to my friend, I looked at her for confirmation and found in her eyes an affirmation that she heard it too. I was not driving that night, so I looked at the driver, the sound growing louder and closer to the car. "We need to get out of here," I said.

We had found what we were looking for, and driving out of there with the lingering sensation of other-worldly things pressing us onwards, we went home.

Over the years, I have had many experiences at this location. None more poignant and frightening than Halloween night when my friends and I piled inside two cars and arrived at the quiet spot expecting nothing more than taps and knocks on our cars. The night was dark and except for the sound of singing crickets and gravel under our feet; beautifully silent. We walked around the area for a while finding nothing. Feeling nothing out of the ordinary, I decided it was time to leave. It was then that Rainer approached me and said, "Jewels, you've got to come here." Walking over to where the other part of the group, I found Mark and another friend holding one of the guests down as she struggled to be free.

Touching her arm, I immediately knew that her hurried and angry resolve to walk into the woods on a dark night was not of her own volition. As well as the fact that her expressions and demeanor had completely changed – and the fact that a 135-pound woman needed at least two strong men to hold her down frightened me deeply. She writhed and screamed while also holding an expression of contempt. I knew then we had to get her out of there fast.

Three people heaved her into the back of the car and we were gone. I can only imagine the how the car ride must have been for those that accompanied her. Even as we left, she demanded by her kicks and screams to be released into those woods. In an effort to calm her down my friends prayed, but they were rebuffed by hisses. When we finally reached my mom's house, she became nauseous and very tired. The next morning when she awoke, she was physically fine and in good spirits. I have no rational explanation for this incident, only that whatever resides in spirit at this location does not always have good intentions.

I must note that I dreamed about this place when I was thirteen years old. In the dream I walk back to an open field bordered by a large windmill and house where I witness a battle between Indians. It was only until several years later when I was exploring the woods around this location that I came to an open field with the same house and windmill. It was as if I was meant to see this place. I do not know why to this day.

I have visited that spot numerous times after these incidents and found it to be a quiet nook for the most part. But if you happen to find it on the right night, you'll likely find that you are not alone. With the crunch of gravel beneath the weight of ghostly feet, and the strange sounds of knocking on your car, I doubt you will stay long.

Little Girl Lost
by Julia Byrd

Wimberley, Texas

Late one night during the summer of 2004, my friends and I decided to stop at a roadside rest stop located about two miles from Ranch Road 12 off of Ranch Road 2325 in Hays County. Pulling into the dark space, the wind on that summer night seemed stronger and cooler than any other places we had previously stopped. I turned off the car and got out with the rest of the group to explore the area. We had decided to go ghost hunting that night, so stopping here only seemed appropriate. After a few minutes of walking around, we sat down at one of the picnic tables and listened for any unexplained noise amid the sound of the breeze through the trees. After about fifteen minutes, we heard the rustling of feet walking on the grass. A black shadow could be seen on the fringes of the rest area. By then, we were satisfied with what we found, so we left.

The next time we visited the rest area I brought a camera and took pictures. We found what appeared to be small orbs on the ground that looked like a ball that a child would play with. After visiting several other times, we discovered more direct interaction with the ghosts – girls there would have their hair stroked, and shiny necklaces would be touched by invisible hands.

Despite the scary reputation that spirits have, for the most part, they are harmless and benevolent. My friends and I learned this in a most unusual way. I usually drove my vehicle on the trips and was a bit nervous about the prospect of a car full of young people out on the back highways in an unreliable car. However, on one of our trips to the rest stop we had taken a friend's car that had experienced some recent engine trouble. The rest stop is desolate and far from the city, so breaking down would be a worse-than-usual problem. I'd had the sickening feel that something bad was going to happen all day long, so needless to say I was on edge.

My apprehension proved correct. We arrived at the rest stop without any duress. However, the moment my friend attempted to restart the car to leave, she could not. We sat there for a good hour, listening to the sounds outside the car, knowing that they might very well be paranormal. The car had cooled down, leaving little doubt that the taps and knocks along with the sound of footsteps pacing around the car were not of this world. We had tried to call others to come to our rescue, but as fate would have it, they could not be reached, or were tied up with something else.

After a while my friend turned they key and the car roared to life. What a relief! We set off down the road with a mission to get home safely. As we were about to reach Megan's house to drop her off, we noticed that a state trooper had pulled over a driver and was giving him a sobriety test. It has always been my belief that the car malfunction was not a product of a faulty part, but that of a spirit seeking to keep us from harm. I honestly believe that if we had left the rest stop when we initially planned, we would have met with some dire circumstances brought on by a drunk driver.

I spoke with a family friend long after this incident and found out that a little girl had drowned in a creek located at the base of the rest stop sometime during the sixties, before the high fence around the rest stop was erected. As well, I had made contact with a young woman named Erin who had been raped and murdered; and whose body had been dumped at that location. After finding a small cross at the base of oak tree a few visits later with the same name inscribed on it, my suspicions about the origin of some of the activity up there were confirmed.

The Pioneer Spirits of Preston Road

by Mitchel Whitington

Dallas, Texas

Preston Road traverses Dallas from north to south, and is traveled by literally thousands of people going about their business, oblivious to its history and the reports of the spirits that might remain there. But could any ghost be brave enough to travel this dangerous byway? After all, on a daily basis, it frightens many of the living... with its traffic, that is.

Preston Road, stretching from downtown Dallas northward to the outer suburbs, is arguably one of the busiest thoroughfares in the Dallas/Fort Worth Metroplex. In fact, publications such as *CNN, Road & Track Magazine*, and *USA Today* have all counted several portions of Preston Road as some of the most dangerous highways in the country. *State Farm Insurance* even weighed in on the subject, naming Preston Road to be one of the Nation's most treacherous thoroughfares. Standing beside the roadway today, it is incredibly hard to imagine how it must have appeared hundreds of years ago.

If you're like me, you probably assume that the road was constructed several decades ago when the city of Dallas began to grow northward. The thoroughfare that we call Preston Road today is older than the city of Dallas, though. Not only that, but it is also older than the State of Texas, the Republic of Texas, and even the United States of America. With something that old, it's no wonder that there are ghost stories associated with it!

Preston Road was originally a pre-Columbian Indian trail, traveled by the ancient people in their journeys to traverse the continent. Later on, the Shawnee tribe adopted it as a path from what is now south Texas to the upper regions of the land. In 1838, the Republic of Texas authorized finances to survey a road from Austin, the Capitol, to the Red River territory. The Shawnee trail was a natural selection, and Colonel W.G. Cooke began the survey in 1840. In October of that year, he crossed the Trinity River – not far from the present-day location of downtown Dallas, and continued north.

The trail that Cooke was surveying led to a military post located near the Red River. The fort was named for Captain William C. Preston, an officer and veteran from the Texas Revolution. Cooke's trail soon became known as "Preston Trail," then "Preston Road," and eventually grew into the frantic highway that it is today.

Still, there may be some remnants of the past holding onto the history of the trail. Ghostly figures have reportedly been seen walking along Preston, especially between Spring Valley and Belt Line Roads. These specters are dressed in clothes of a century past, and are making their way north, as if on a twilight trek to Fort Preston.

I can't imagine how anyone would notice them with all of the traffic whizzing by, but I decided to give the spirits a chance. All in all, I made three trips to Preston Road to look for ghosts: one on a Saturday afternoon, when the traffic was moderate; another on an early Tuesday morning just in time for rush hour; the final one I made just before midnight to find a time when the traffic had thinned out considerably. On each of the occasions, I walked the shoulder between Spring Valley and Belt Line, hoping to see some of the pioneer spirits. It was a nice little hike – who says that ghost hunting isn't good exercise!

The rush hour visit was just plain crazy. I spent more time worrying that I was going to be nailed by some passing automobile than looking for ghosts, and if you've ever traveled that road in the early morning, you know what I mean. I don't think that I've ever seen so many people in such a hurry! I feel compelled at this point to recommend against trying this yourself. It's not for the faint of heart.

The most interesting visit was the late evening trek. There were fewer cars, and I was able to actually stop and reflect on the history of Preston Road. If nothing else, it was very interesting to imagine that I was walking in the very footsteps of ancient bands of Indians as they headed northward. While I was doing this, something interesting happened. I was crossing over a bridge, and caught a glimpse of something on the other side of the road. I'd like to say that it was grayish, and moving in the opposite direction that I was, but it was just a peripheral sight out of the corner of my eye. When I turned my head there was nothing there – most likely, it was the moonlight reflecting of the bridge's metal railing, or the glimmer of an approaching car's headlights.

The most entertaining visit was on a Saturday afternoon. After making a non-eventful trek along the roadside, I stopped into a burger joint to get a soft drink. Two Dallas police officers were seated inside, having a late lunch, so I decided to get the opinion of someone who drove Preston Road for a living. After procuring a diet cola, I approached the officers and introduced myself. There's just no elegant way to broach the subject, so I dove right in: "I'm doing research for a book about haunted places in North Texas, and I've been told that Preston Road has a few ghosts that walk along the highway in dressed in pioneer clothing. Have you guys ever heard of anything like that?"

They looked at me, glanced at each other, and then both kind of smiled before one of them replied, "You mean *real* ghosts? Out on Preston Road?"

"Yep, right out there. I've walked the roadsides between Spring Valley and Belt Line, but haven't had any supernatural experience at all. I just wondered if you guys have ever seen anything like a ghost beside the road, or had any reports like that."

The officer laughed, and said, "If you're not careful out there, you may be the next ghost, with the way that some of those people drive!"

We had a nice visit, and even though they were interested in the ghost story, and asked a lot of questions about the book, neither had heard nor seen anything that could be of help with the Preston Road ghosts.

It was a little frustrating, and I was starting to wonder how the Ghosts of Preston Road stacked up against known fraudulent ghost stories such as the Lady of White Rock Lake, or the Screaming Bridge, both of which are covered in other chapters in this book. The one thing that kept me interested in this tale was that I did find multiple sources of information about it, but none of them contradicted each other, as did the different versions of the White Rock Lady. There were also no telltale signs of high-school legends, such as honking your horn at a certain time or place like in the Screaming Bridge stories. Of course, that still doesn't lend any extra credibility to the Preston Road Ghosts, but it doesn't send up any red flags either.

I went home, and got on an online supernatural chat site just to see if I could locate anyone who'd seen the spirits. Although many people had heard of the ghosts, no one online at the time had actually experienced them. One fellow was even proclaiming that he was going to drive over to Preston Road to see if he could find them – but unfortunately, spirits work on their own schedules, not ours. It was no surprise to me when he posted a follow-up note saying that there were no ghosts there when he drove by.

I was just about to shut the computer down when one fellow told me that he'd heard that the ghosts were "corner people" – ghosts that you'd catch in the corner of your eye. It made me rethink what I'd seen that evening on the bridge – maybe it hadn't been a reflection after all, or perhaps it was just wishful thinking on my part.

In any case, no one seems to know who these spirits are. From all reports, they seem oblivious to the traffic rushing by, and they'd have to be to choose Preston Road as place for an Earthly appearance. If you are driving down Preston, however, and happen to catch the glimpse of these wandering figures as the sun starts to set on North Dallas, there is no need to stop. They'll be gone before you can even turn your head completely, even though they continue on some perpetual northern journey.

The Raggedy Man
by Julia Byrd

San Marcos, Texas

With the onset of night, the tranquil winding byways of the Texas Hill Country darken into a mysterious world. It is there in the shadows of the trees, as the moon rolls through the clouds, that unexplained sounds and shadows make the hairs of the human body stand on end with fear of the unknown. Any unexplainable happenings can only hearken to the history of the area once filled with the chaos of war and the silent toil of hardships. In this area, we are never alone, even if our eyes cannot see the intruders among us. Or perhaps, we are the visitors intruding the world of the dead?

Purgatory Road is a winding byway that connects Farm to Market Road 306 in Comal County to Ranch Road 12 in Hays County, and holds testament to the changing shape of the Texas Hill Country. In close proximity to San Marcos, the area is both a mixture of new and old, as evidenced the rusty fences and crumbling rock walls set against the gleaming pavement. Among these pockets of history, one can find an old cemetery just off the road surrounded by a rust-covered fence and a thick canopy of large oak and cedar trees. It is easy to miss this small area located just after a stretch of winding road and before the end of Purgatory Road. Once you find the location, you will never forget it.

I had just completed my freshman year at Texas Lutheran University, and with school out, my friends and I itched for something different to do during the cool summer nights. Being young with little to do in the small town of Canyon Lake, we opted to go ghost haunting, knowing that soon or later something would scare us senseless. With this singular mission in mind, we piled into my mom's Dodge Caravan and made way to the cemetery. The night was dark, and there was a feeling of foreboding as we pulled up to the entrance. When we turned off the engine, we sat there momentarily, still inside the car, afraid to move. Woody was the first to speak up and the first to get out. He took pictures of the cemetery entrance, then moved to the fence line and snapped pictures of the headstones while the rest of us sat there and waited for him to finish. I had always fancied myself sensitive to the paranormal, having had experiences since I was a child, so I opted to stay inside the car. I knew that something was there and was not anxious to find out what it was.

Later that evening, when we got back to my house, we uploaded all the pictures that Woody took and were stunned to find a face with two red eyes in one of the pictures. Even more frightening was the fact that this had been the very first picture he had snapped that night. There was not a streetlight in the near proximity to have created the effect of two eyes. Woody had also noted that the temperature around the fence line had been noticeably cooler. Woody took the picture many years later and sent it to The Atlantic Paranormal Society (TAPS). After enhancing it, they apparently found the picture just as startling, making sure to ask where we took it, and comments about how freaky it was.

With that experience and picture in mind, my friends and I have made more visits to the cemetery. One time in particular, we had arrived at the cemetery and were immediately aware of a presence. Turning off the engine and leaving the headlights on, I could see the formation of a pant leg in motion. It was if a man paced back and forth along the fence. Over the course of a minute, more of his pants leg became apparent, till his bottom half was almost complete. Not wanting to stick around any longer, I started the car, threw it into reverse, and then sped away.

Not to be ousted from my now-favorite ghost hunting spot, I visited the location again with a van full of my friends late on a Saturday night. Pulling up to the entrance, a presence was felt immediately. Nobody got out of the car; we were still and quiet as church mice, waiting for a sound or apparition to appear. Our patience was rewarded because as we sat there, we heard the sound of running water outside the car. The sense of being stalked pervaded the air, and with the increasing tension, we screamed when something knocked twice on the window. Mind you, the only people present were inside the car – the sound could have only been made if someone was knocking from the outside.

When you sit outside the cemetery entrance in your car on a still night, you can see the grass moving, as if someone is walking through it. Conversely, you might also hear movements in the thick brush, although the blades of glass remain still.

After visiting the cemetery over the course of a year, I found that it was not uncommon to find the gate open as if to beckon me inside so that I could see the rest of the spirits. There are multiple entities there and they vary in age range. Most of the graves are unmarked and all of the people buried there seem to be related.

The surnames of some of the deceased are: Clayton, Williamson, and Allen. In the late 1800s this area was known as the Hugo Township. Most of the graves date back to the 1880s and the turn of the last century; however there is one grave there that belongs to a Confederate soldier. The principle spirit, who seems to be the self-appointed guardian of the cemetery, is a six-foot three-inch old-timer commonly referred to as the "raggedy man." He wears long khaki pants, a white short-sleeved dress shirt with suspenders and a hat. So, if you decide to visit, take care to be respectful and never enter the actual cemetery unless invited by an open gate.

During the course of our visits to the cemetery, my friends and I never entered, letting the raggedy man take the initiative to approve our presence inside that sacred place. He is an intelligent spirit that will not easily forget those who decide to visit, so if you are passing by one day and feel his eyes, you know he is waiting for you to come and make his acquaintance.

The Devil's Backbone

by Tammy Petty Conrad

Wimberley, Texas

Why would anyone want to travel down a road known by the nickname *The Devil's Backbone*? I don't know, because it seems that this part of the Texas Hill Country is famous for much more than its panoramic vistas.

North of San Antonio, Ranch Road 32 runs east to west linking Ranch Road 12 and U.S. Highway 281 between Wimberley and Blanco. It is an especially scenic drive on the way to Canyon Lake for summer boaters, those who enjoy perusing area antique shops, or even for folks eager to spend the weekend in a quaint bed and breakfast. Occasionally these visitors have an unexpected bonus... a ghostly encounter.

A variety of spirits have been reported in the area and the characters date as far back as Spanish monks from the 1500s, but also include Native American Indians and Confederate soldiers. Interestingly enough, the Spanish name for the area *Espinoza Diablo*, which translates as *Devil's Backbone*, is thought to come from the monk who traveled with the Spaniards as they explored the area. The monk was especially cruel and the soldiers did not enjoy his company – perhaps this is who visitors speak of appearing briefly, as if out of thin air.

One ranch owner, Bert Wall, has written a book detailing the many sightings on his land. His stories have been featured on several television programs. In his book *Ghost Stories from the Texas Hill Country*, Mr. Wall recounts his own sightings as well as those visitors have shared with him. No one has ever been harmed by an apparition, but many have been so scared that they never returned to the area. Reading his book definitely made me want to take a drive through the region for myself. I wasn't brave enough to attempt any such adventure at night, however, which is when the visions most often materialize.

Most of the sightings appear off the highway, but there have been glimpses of a woman dressed in white on Ranch Road 12 less than ten miles outside of Wimberley. What does she want? Would I be so distracted that I might crash my car? My fears and vivid imagination have kept me from making a nighttime visit. But thinking of the history of the area, it is not hard to imagine all the suffering souls who have been left behind to traverse the land where they lost their lives.

It is actually quite a vast area with over 4,000 acres and elevations reaching approximately 1,000 feet in places. The Comanche and Apache Indians inhabited this area in the 1800s and their interactions with the incoming settlers and each other were not always peaceful. Of course, the settlers themselves caused their own violence at times as well.

If I do ever find myself in the area after dark, I will definitely choose an alternate route to my destination... just to be on the safe side!

Possessed by the Spirit of a Wolf

by Robert Fears

San Marcos, Texas

A wolf's spirit is said to be free, committed to survival, protective of his territory and unafraid to face his enemies. Native Americans admire the wolf because of his cunning, patience, and perseverance. A wolf moves silently without effort, but with purpose. Many feel that the wolf's spirit is ever-present, and some claim that it can take control of your body and mind.

This concept is frequently discussed by people who live on and visit the Devil's Backbone in Central Texas. The Devil's Backbone is a range of large hills, located between San Marcos and Blanco and provides some of the most beautiful scenery in Texas. An average tourist, who travels Ranch Road 32 along the top of the Backbone, only becomes aware of its steep hillsides, deep canyons and valleys covered with mantles of green cedar and oak. Many local people, however, say that this rough, majestic terrain is home to spirits from the past. They will tell you that the spirit of the wolf is very active and takes different forms and shapes. People who have ventured into private lands off the highway can attest to seeing ghosts of priests, outlaws, women, and children.

History tells us that some of the first people to occupy canyons and valleys of the Devil's Backbone were Apaches, later joined by Comanche. One of the first Spanish explorers to arrive on the Devil's Backbone was General Miranda who was searching for a legendary city of gold. His troops were accompanied by a priest named Espinoza. It was recorded that Espinoza was greedy, mean and very cruel to laborers. At his direction, the Spaniards enslaved Indians who retaliated by going on the warpath. The Indians quickly drove the Spaniards from the Backbone and they did not return. Espinoza's apparition, dressed in a gray robe with a crucifix hung on a sash at his waist, has been seen at ranch houses on several occasions. Attempts to approach him have resulted in his spirit floating away.

When Spanish land grants were issued to European and United States immigrants, some of them settled in fertile areas around the Backbone. Feeling hemmed in, the Comanche began a campaign to drive out the settlers as well as the Apaches. Apaches, who wanted to defend their burial grounds and other sacred sites within the valleys and hills, joined with white settlers to fight the Comanche. Comanche succeeded in routing the Apaches and then were later beaten and placed on reservations by the federal army.

These two tribes, who always strived to develop abilities of the wolf, are said to still linger as spirits in canyons and on hillsides of the Devil's Backbone to protect their sacred grounds. It has been reported on more than one occasion that Indian ghosts have appeared before contractors who were building roads, ponds, or other structures.

Although they did not talk, these spirits were able to communicate that construction must be stopped and it was. It has also been said that Indian spirits have ushered hikers, ranchers, and other visitors away from their sacred areas. Many of these spirits wore feathered headdresses of a chief and carried old repeater rifles.

During the Civil War and the ensuing reconstruction period, the Devil's Backbone harbored outlaws, cattle rustlers, and others hiding from the law. These outcasts, mostly men, were cunning, silent, and swift and would fight to the death for what they claimed as theirs. They lived like wolves and appeared to have their spirit. Apparitions of these desperados, including John Wesley Harding and Frank and Jesse James, have been seen at different times in remote areas of the Backbone wearing long coats and worn leather holsters containing pearl-handle pistols. Some of their spirits appear when people go near areas where stolen money is thought to be hidden while others seem to want to amend their bad deeds by saving others.

One attempt of an outlaw spirit to atone for previous misdeeds occurred at a Boy Scout camp located at the south end of Devil's Backbone. One night a group of boys decided to sneak from camp and explore along the Blanco River. When they reached the river they were met by a tall, weather-beaten man wearing worn, dusty leather boots with big rowel spurs, faded pants, and a long gray coat. His head was covered with a sweat-streaked felt hat with a wide brim bent down over his eyes. Although he did not speak loudly the scouts heard his message, "Leave now." The scouts immediately scurried up the riverbank, ran to camp, and jumped into their tents closing the flaps behind them.

Within a short time, a wall of water came rushing down the river from a flash flood upstream. If the boys had not left, they would have drowned.

Many farmers who settled in surrounding counties had migrated from the Southern United States cotton belt and were slave owners. When the Civil War broke out, they joined the Confederacy so it was not uncommon for Confederate troops to travel along the Devil's Backbone. Some of these troops were companies of raiders including Quantrill and his band. These raiders lived like wolves, silently tracking their prey, attacking swiftly and effectively, and then melting back into hills and brush. Although the Confederacy lost the war, some raiders did not surrender and continued to fight, even after death. Cowboys in the Backbone have heard a thundering roar of mounted horseman riding through ranch headquarters and have seen apparitions of gray-coated riders.

In addition to cowboys, prospectors tunneled into the hillsides of the Devil's Backbone in search of gold and silver. Improperly braced mine shafts frequently collapsed leaving a miner trapped. Often the miner had a family waiting for him to return home in the evening. When the miner did not appear, his family initiated a frantic search and in many instances, the miner was not found. Spirits of these grieving women have been seen searching for their husbands. A woman wearing a white grown and accompanied by a big gray wolf has appeared along Ranch Road 32. This pair has been known to follow a car for several miles and then disappear.

People claim that the spirit of the wolf is still active on the Devil's Backbone.

Present-day hunters, hikers, and residents have reported being captured in trances when they approached the area that is thought to be protected by the spirit of the wolf. These trances left talkative and jovial people suddenly silent and incoherent. When they did talk, it was in a husky, bass voice totally atypical to their normal tone. Sometimes these trances would last only minutes, sometimes hours, and on rare instances, several days. After recovering from this experience, the person never wanted to return to the area where it occurred.

Travel across the Devil's Backbone is highly recommended because of its natural beauty. But if a stranger invites you to visit one of the ranches, be careful where you go and, most of all, be sure you were not invited by a ghost.

The Hanging Tree

by Julia Byrd

New Braunfels, Texas

On a quiet evening, my friends and I decided to pack into a small car in hopes of finding a good scare on a dark country road. We had exhausted our other spots without luck, so we decided to transverse down Roller Roaster Road and try again. Roller Coaster Road, located ten minutes from New Braunfels and off of Farm to Market Road 306, is fun to drive and better known to non-locals as Hoffman Lane. Over the course of the many years that I have resided in the Texas Hill Country, there had been several accidents with fatalities on that road.

The turbulent history of the area with the localized Indian wars and fighting between Indians and pioneers made the area ripe for paranormal activity. I knew this, but more importantly, I remembered a strange story that my mother had told me about the area.

The experience of a property owner's son along Hoffman Lane was relayed to my mom when my parents were looking at buying some land on which to build the family home. As the story goes, the son and his friend were walking late one night in the backwoods of the man's property, disbelieving of the father's warnings about Indian paranormal activity. Coming into a wash bathed in the cool glow of the full moon, they suddenly found themselves in the heat of a battle between two Indian tribes. The scene was as plain as day and perfectly clear in detail, from the brave's war paint to the sounds of tomahawks and war-cries. The young men watched in disbelief. It was only when they were noticed by some of the braves and chased out of the wash that they finally heeded their father's warning to stay out of the area.

As luck would have it, the thick fog, heavy humidity and still air offered the perfect scene for our own real-life thriller. We stopped just yards away from a new development project under the darkness of an old oak tree, turned the ignition off and waited for a noise.

Nothing happened for a solid twenty minutes. Anxious for the possibility of finding a scare someplace else, we decided it was time to leave. My senses would not let me leave, however, unless I turned and looked down the driveway adjacent to our parked car. I had been quiet for most of the night, opting to observe first rather than simply freak out when, and if, we encountered paranormal activity.

When we initially stopped at this location, I began to feel a dull pain in the back of my head that traveled down my spine and intensified with each passing moment. Activity seemed to be coming from beside us in the pasture. I turned my head and peered into the darkness behind a sagging fence, and spotted something hanging from a large oak tree. On such a still night, I was surprised that the human form slowly swayed back and forth. Thinking that my eyes were deceiving me, I peered at it for what seemed like a good five minutes before I turned to Woody who was sitting beside me in the back seat. He validated with just a look and a simple question, "Do you see that?" Priscilla and Theresa in the front seat were able to dismiss the figure as a simple Halloween decoration, while Megan, Woody and I in the back seat knew better. Seeking some concrete validation for the skeptics in the front seat, I turned and looked out of the window once again. I noticed that there was a rather large gravestone directly beneath the swaying figure. This was the perfect incentive to finally leave, as the dull ache had heavily sunk into my body and I was beginning to fall into a sleep-like state. Priscilla and Theresa were anxious to go, because they were bored and didn't believe any of our observations in the back seat. Still, what we had seen seemed like a good enough reason to leave. Theresa started the car, put it in gear and we proceeded on without a look back to the swinging body. Megan, Woody and I were grateful. The heaviness of that feeling from the dead man stayed with us even as we drove back to my mom's house.

We decided to go back to the spot the next day and investigate whether or not the figure we'd seen was a Halloween decoration – after all, it was the fall season and near October 31st.

As we pulled up to the spot where we had been to the night before, we were chilled to discover nothing hanging from the tree. Those who had been so skeptical fell into a deep silence that remained even as we drove away. We could not get close to the tombstone, as it was secured behind a gate, and knowing that our trespassing might be greeted by a shotgun, we opted not to go into the fenced area. The man whose life was taken and whose name was carved on the stone would not be known. Only the gravestone and the memory of our previous encounter remained, leaving us with the haunting reminder of death's indelible mark on the landscape of the Texas Hill Country.

Indian Lookout

by Bettey Baldwin

San Antonio, Texas

The Native American spirit out near Indian Lookout probably has a hard time getting noticed nowadays. When I was a kid, Nacogdoches Street ran east from the heart of San Antonio to the city limits. There it became a country road that ran by the quarry and eventually ran into Highway 81 (the old Austin highway).

San Antonio is the second oldest European settlement in the United States and it has a lot of ghosts. The one prowling around out near Indian Lookout didn't attract that much attention when my cousins, friends and I were trying to scare the bejebus out of each other telling ghost stories at night.

In August of 1954, I saw Indian Lookout for the first time. There were half a dozen of us kids packed into a car that was older than any of us. Our mothers were in the front seat. Those old cars had a lot of room in them and we'd never heard of seat belts in those days. The only safety tip that we heard was, "Don't stick your head out the window. A passing truck might lop it off." Since this was the road to the quarry, trucks often whizzed past on the two-lane, no-shoulder road.

A single hill stood sentinel quite a ways out in the country. The big house built on top of it commanded a view of the surrounding countryside for miles and miles. The house was surrounded by a rock wall, and each gatepost had a carved head

141

of a Plains Indian on top of it. None of this meant much to me at the time – I was far more interested in the end of our journey at Landa Park in New Braunfels. I was going to get to swim in a real swimming pool for the first time in my life. For most of my life, the pools had been closed because of polio.

My mother's favorite thing in New Braunfels was the cotton mills along the Landa River which made a huge variety of cotton cloth at very cheap prices. It became a tradition to go shopping for material to make school clothes and let the kids swim after the shopping trip providing we didn't destroy the stores.

Indian Lookout was the halfway marker we kids kept an eye out for every time we went to New Braunfels.

I'd gawk a bit at the hill with its house and Indian heads as we drove along. It wasn't until my seventh grade, during Texas history, that I learned the hill was called Indian Lookout, not because of the heads on the gateposts, but because for several centuries Spanish, French, Mexican, Texan and United States settlers used the hill to keep a lookout for Indians.

Indians inhabited the area because, at that time, great herds of buffalo and other game roamed the area. More importantly than game were the springs that provided abundant water in a dry land. Some of those springs can still be observed at Landa Park in New Braunfels, and at San Pedro Park in San Antonio.

Long before Europeans came into the area conflict arose over who would have access to these springs. Even today after heavy rains, it's possible to find arrowheads near these springs. Spear heads and hand axes dating back thousands of years have also been discovered near these springs. With millennia of conflict over the precious resource of water it would be more wonderful if ghosts weren't seen nearby.

Even before State Loop 1604 was built there were occasional reports of an Indian seen in the area. He was dressed in moccasins, leggings, loincloth, and had feathers in his breads. ? Since no one ever reported war paint, it is probably not the ghost of a warrior.

Shortly after that section of State Loop 1604 was opened, there was a auto pile up and the truck drivers who caused the mess swore they'd hit the brakes because a man dressed like an Indian ran across the road in front of them. Two different drivers apparently saw the apparition that time, which validated the experience. Other similar sightings have usually involved only one person.

These days Indian Lookout is a city-maintained park. It no longer has the house, walls, or gateposts. There are trails leading to the top of the hill where you can still get a good view of the surrounding countryside. Only now instead of plains with grasses and brush there are shopping centers and housing developments; all with Lookout in their names. In the distance are a Wal-Mart and a mall. Nacogdoches Street is now a four-lane road with constant traffic. The Indian hunter may still be out there, but the chances of seeing him are probably much less likely than they were fifty years ago. Still, if you are out walking your dog at night, you just might get lucky and see something that you don't quite believe out of the corner of your eye.

The Children of the Ghost Tracks – Fact or Fiction?

by Dede Harper

San Antonio, Texas

Certainly a book about Texas ghosts and haunts would not be complete without the mention of one of the most famous ghost legends in the state, "The Children of the Ghost Tracks." In fact, this legend has garnered so much attention that even a popular cable television show has found its way to the intersection of Villamain Road and the Southern Pacific Railroad in southern Bexar County in order to cover the legend. And, thus, unceremoniously debunk it.

The story definitely embodies the stuff of good folklore, and that is exactly what this story is, because at this point, no real evidence has been found to prove an accident involving children ever occurred. However, new historical data has been found that shows parts of the tale indeed might be true.

According to one version of the legend sometime in the 1940s or the 1950s, a school bus carrying children stalled on the railroad tracks late one afternoon at the intersection of Villamain Road and Shane Road. A horrendous accident resulted when a freight train came through and smashed into the hindered vehicle. All aboard the bus lost their lives that day and it is the spirits of these children that haunt the area.

The legend further describes how the haunting takes place. If you go to that intersection and stop your car fifty yards or so from the tracks on Villamain Road, then put the car in neutral and take your foot off of the brake and accelerator, your car will begin to roll toward the tracks. It will continue up and over a small incline and finally pass over the tracks themselves. The force driving the car toward the track is the spirits of the dead children pushing on the vehicle as they guard the area, preventing other accidents from occurring there. The legend further suggests that if you dust your car with flour or talcum powder before you cross the intersection, you will find tiny handprints left on your car from the spirits of the children after crossing the tracks.

Also near the accident sight is a housing subdivision, McCreeless Meadows, where the street names are supposedly named after the dead children. Such names include Shane Road, Cindy Sue, Bobbie Allen, Richey Otis, Nancy Carole and Laura Lee Way.

One would think that if the streets were named after the accident victims then we could find evidence of an accident around this timeframe?

On my hunt to find factual evidence to back up the legend, I became quite familiar with the historical maps available on the internet. The ones I accessed in San Antonio provided by the State of Texas Freeway site do not even show a listing for Villamain Road before 1960. However that could be because the intersection is located on the outskirts of the city, close to State Loop 410. In fact upon further investigation via the Bexar County Appraisal District, I found the first houses in the McCreeless Meadows Subdivision were built in the early 1960s. According to the *San Antonio Express News*, the names of the streets came from the names of the children of the builder of the subdivision and not from the victims of a train wreck.

Still the legend lives on today and it probably has more to do with the locale than anything else. The intersection itself is wooded and not well lit. Calling it creepy would certainly fit. Bones of a woman were found in the area back in August of 1995 and the body of another woman was found along Shane Road in March of 2006. Thrill-seeking teenagers have always gravitated to the area as far back as the 1950s when the intersection was referred to as "Roller Coaster Road." Some people have reported encountering interesting experiences at the sight. One man reported seeing an apparition in the area in the form of a little girl. Others have said they heard moans and cries of terror coming from the fabled intersection.

The police have tried to curtail the excursions to the area by tourists and thrill-seekers largely because it is not considered a safe area. There are no streetlamps around. Gangs of youths have been known to hide in the woods and rob those who leave their car to check for fingerprints. The railroad tracks are still not marked with any type of crossing arm and are considered hazardous. With all of this said and known, the legend continues to entice the crowds, especially around Halloween, when hundreds descend on the area hoping to be pushed to safety by the dead children.

Another version of the story has the accident taking place sometime in the 1930s but it was a truck full of children that got hit on their way to school. With this account of the legend, we can find some proof. The story I found in the *Dallas Morning News* archives shows many similarities to this version of the tale but there's one very important aspect that differs.

According to an article appearing in the April 23, 1934 edition of the *Dallas Morning News*, the bodies of four children were mangled with "bits being strewn along the railroad" when a Missouri-Kansas-Texas passenger train collided with a truck, also referred to in the article as a Sunday school bus. Three other children and the driver of the converted bus were hurt less seriously as they made their way to Sunday school at the Harlandale Presbyterian Church located in San Antonio that day. If the accident isn't enough to make you cringe, then the other sensational aspect of this story certainly will. Three of the four dead children were from the same family: Sylven Book age 14, Mary Book age 5, and Wenfred Book age 12.

And the one very important difference between this reality and the tall tale? This horrible accident between the truck or "improvised bus" and the Katy Flyer occurred at the intersection of Probandt Street and the railroad line, and not at Villamain Road.

After researching this article, I found the tragedy of the accident has not diminished over the years. I think perhaps it is more credible to let legend live on at Villamain Road, knowing an accident of this nature has never occurred there, instead of knowing the truth: that indeed the gruesome death of four children took place just a little bit farther north.

Bandera Pass

by Dede Harper

Bandera, Texas

In the Texas Hill Country there is a vital parcel of land that borders the counties of Bandera and Kerr with access to two water sources, the Guadalupe and the Medina rivers. The valley that lies between these two rivers is known as Bandera Pass, or in Spanish as *Puerto de la Bandera*. It is also called Gorge of the Flag, or simply "the Pass," this beautiful area, rich in natural resources, is reported to be haunted by not one but several ghosts.

The Pass itself is one hundred yards wide and five hundred yards long. Originally a trail ran through it but today it is marked by State Highway 173, which begins in the city of Devine, located in Medina County, and stops at the intersection of State Highway 16 just south of Kerrville in Kerr County. It is surrounded by some of the most picturesque land in Texas, and it's not uncommon to see travelers stop along the highways to picnic in the spring and summer months.

It is easy to imagine the beauty of the area with its bountiful wildflowers and wild game effortlessly supported by the fertile river valleys cutting through the limestone bluffs. It is also easy to understand why men have fought over it for centuries. More than one culture of people has shared this land, and not always in peace. In fact, some of the most chilling and bloodthirsty battles between clashing cultures have occurred

148

within the walls of the Pass. With as much death as the region has seen, is it any wonder why the Pass is thought to be haunted? Several ghostly legends abound from the area. However, to even begin to believe in this land's ghostly connections, it is important to know about its bloody past.

The Guadalupe River, named for Our Lady of Guadalupe by Spanish explorer Alonzo de Leon in 1689, runs two hundred and fifty miles long. It supported one of the first Spanish settlements in Texas, then later one of the first Anglo-American settlements in the state. Of course the area sustained several Native American tribes long before the first colonists arrived.

According to early maps derived by explorers in the early 1800s, a large Apache Rancheria sat just north of the Pass. The Comanche also used the Pass because it lay along the old Comanche Trail leading from Nacogdoches. Swiss Botanist Jean Louis Berlander, a member of a Mexican scientific expedition in 1828, described in John C. Ewers' 1969 book, *The Indians of Texas in 1830* by Jean Louis Berlander, how Bandera Pass was a holy ground to Native Americans:

Here a Comanche warrior was buried, and since the natives often pass this way, every tribe that passes close enough to see the grave of one of their ancestors makes the customary offerings. On the grave they place arrows, bows, sundry weapons, enemy trophies, and the like, and even sacrifice mules and horses to his shade. The gorge, which is known for this custom, is strewn with the bones of the animals that have been sacrificed here. The grave itself is surrounded with skulls.

Legend has it that the name "Bandera" was given to the area after intense fighting between Indians and Spanish soldiers protecting the settlements around San Antonio in Bexar County. Some say soldiers pursued the raiding Indians through the Pass then planted a flag in there to remind the Indians not to come any closer unless they wanted to be pursued to the death.

Other accounts show a man by the name of Manuel Bandera owning property at the junction of the Arroyo de Alazán and the Arroyo de San Pedro near Nuestra Señora de la Purísima Concepción de Acuña Mission at San Antonio. Perhaps the area was named after him. Some sources theorize he might have been a general in the Spanish Army who fought the Indians during this time but this story cannot be corroborated.

The early Spanish settlers used the Pass as an easy yet risky route from Bexar to the mission outpost at San Saba. Historical documents show Stephen F. Austin designating the creek bed running into Medina River as Puerto de la Bandera in a map he presented to the Mexican government back in 1829.

Further bloody battles and chases ensued through the Pass. In 1843 the Comanche ambushed Texas Ranger John Coffee Hays and his ranger outfit as they crossed through the Pass. Hays and his unit fought valiantly for well over an hour until the Indians withdrew. Later, Hays confessed that the new technology of their five shot Colt revolvers saved them from annihilation. Today this event in history is commemorated by a Texas Centennial Marker.

In the 1850s soldiers and settlers frequently used the pass to go between the lumber camp on the Medina called Bandera and the new cavalry post of Camp Verde. Postal service began in the area via the Pony Express. In such an area formed and fought over by men on horseback, it is almost logical to think that a headless horseman haunts the Pass.

According to folklorist William J. Campion in his book, *The Lore and Legend of the Texas Hill Country,* Ben, a Pony Express rider, rode from Castroville through Bandera in Bandera County and then onto Kerrville in Kerr County as part of his typical route. However, at the end of this day's journey something exciting would take place. His sweetheart, Sarah, waited for him in Kerrville to become his bride.

The first day he rode from Castroville to Bandera and did not encounter any problems. On the second day, when he came upon Bandera Pass, the story goes at a fantastic feeling of foreboding took over. Soon after, a band of Indians, some say renegade Comanche and others say Apache, swooped down on him. Ben fought hard, annihilating as many Indians as he could, but alas, a final arrow pierced his heart. Because he had killed so many Indians that day, those left alive were not satisfied with just killing him; they cut off his head as well.

When Ben did not arrive with the mail, a posse formed and went out searching for him. They found his body and brought it back to town. Sarah went crazy after hearing of Ben's death. She forced the posse to show her the massacre site where she proclaimed that Ben's ghost would forever defend the pass and that Indians would no longer raid nor ransack there. Local lore suggests that no more attacks ever occurred. In fact, the Indians avoided the pass altogether because of the "crazy squaw's curse." Thus the legend of the headless horseman of Bandera Pass began.

On nights when the sky is lit by the stars and the moon, travelers have witnessed a headless horseman protecting the Pass. The gallop of hooves can be heard as the valiant ghost tends to his duty.

Another version of the headless horseman tale does not mention Sarah or Ben, but states that a decapitated man mounted on a white horse haunts the area between Bandera Pass and Center Point. When travelers come upon pools of blood, the headless horseman appears and chases them through the pass, then, poof, disappears.

Other legends suggest it is not a headless horseman that haunts the Pass but a ghost wagon of settlers murdered by Apache Indians. This apparition has appeared in some of the local ranchers' fields over the years.

Still another legend states that lights can be seen in and around the Pass similar to those seen in Marfa. Supposedly these "ghost lights" are the spirits of settlers from the 1800s protecting a lost treasure they hid from Indians.

In the twenty-first century, the violent history of Bandera Pass has become a thing of the past, but the beauty of the area remains. While the breathtaking splendor of the Guadalupe and Medina river valleys is worth a look, a drive through the Pass and the chance encounter of a ghostly legend is more than worth a thousand pictures.

Haunted Goliad
by Vivian Kirkbride

Goliad, Texas

The spirits of Goliad cry to us, moan to us, and remind us that when a human life meets a violent end, the spirit might not be able to rest. One of the most horrifying events that happened during the Texas Battle for Independence occurred in South Texas, at the Presidio La Bahia in Goliad, on U.S. Highway 183. On Palm Sunday, March 27, 1836, Mexico's General Santa Anna's forces encountered Colonel James Walker Fannin and 352 unarmed men, and shot them down in cold blood.

Shots rang out in the early morning air, mingling gun smoke with fog. Screams, groans, and death hovered over the area.

Today, Goliad is shrouded with the overwhelming magnitude of human suffering and sorrow. Visitors to Goliad are haunted by cold spots, feelings of being watched, and the eerie crying of infants coming from unmarked graves in the old, 1700s cemetery. Goose pimples are common in Goliad.

Goliad is the 3rd oldest settlement in Texas, first named Santa Dorotea, by the Spanish in the 16th century. In 1749, Presidio La Bahia was firmly established at the site of a small Aranama Indian village. It served as one of the most important Spanish settlements in Texas. Mexican soldiers occupied the Presidio from 1821 to 1825. Soon after Mexico gained independence from Spain, the name was changed to Goliad in 1829.

Goliad sat at a strategic location during the Texas Revolution, a place desired by both Mexico and Texas. On Oct. 9, 1835, local Texans captured the fort and town from the Mexicans. This led to the signing of the first Declaration of Texas Independence on the altar of the Presidio chapel on December 20, 1835.

Mid-March 1836, Texas Colonel Fannin learned that Mexico's General Urrea and approximately 1,700 professional soldiers were crossing the Rio Grande, marching up the Texas Gulf coast to recapture Goliad.

Fannin knew the Alamo had already fallen and that he was severely outnumbered. He knew that when men stood up to General Urrea at San Patrico, Texan bodies were left behind for the coyotes and wolves to dispose of. The times were troubled and turbulent – Fannin had to either stand and fight, or retreat.

They tried to retreat, but Urrea trapped them on the open plain, cutting them off from Coleto Creek. Men and animals fell on the battleground. Wounded men moaned, crying for water. Urrea's side sustained as many as 400 casualties. Fannin took a bullet in the thigh.

Hoping to relieve suffering and to save the lives of his men, Colonel Fannin ran up a white flag and surrendered on March 20, 1836.

Urrea assured the Texans that they would be shipped back to the United States as soon as possible. Fannin believed that his men would be treated well as prisoners of war and signed an agreement to that effect. They turned over their rifles, 500 spare muskets, and nine brass cannons.

Prisoners were marched to Goliad, where the men suffered overcrowding and vile food.

Urrea sent a letter to Colonel Portilla at the Presidio to treat Fannin's men with consideration and respect. But Santa Anna, a cunning and cruel man, sent orders to execute them.

Under heavy guard, at around 8 a.m. on a foggy morning, approximately 342 able-bodied Texans were marched in three columns down the Baxter Road, San Patrico Road, and the Victoria Road. The unsuspecting Texans were told they would gather wood, or drive cattle, or go to the port of Copano. Unarmed, they believed they would eventually be set free. On Palm Sunday, March 27, 1836, Colonel Portilla's Mexican soldiers fulfilled Santa Anna's order.

At preselected spots on each of the three roads defenseless Texans were shot, bayoneted and clubbed to death a few yards from the fort. Shots rang out, musketry echoed across the prairie with the sounds of a second volley. The blood of the Texans spilled as men convulsed in their last agony. Massacred.

The Mexican soldiers returned to the fort and executed the wounded men, who were in the chapel. They saved Colonel Fannin for last.

Bodies were piled high and set on fire. Fannin and his troops suffered violent deaths; their bodies stripped, and left unburied emphasized the dishonorable execution.

The Angel of Goliad, Panchita Alvarez, wife of a high-ranking officer in the Mexican army is credited with saving at least twenty-eight men, by begging the commander to spare them. Another twenty-eight men managed to escape the firing squads. Only twenty were spared because they had skills the Mexican army needed.

Two months later, on June 3, 1836, General Rusk found the bodies that had been burned, and exposed to vultures and coyotes. The remains were buried with military honors in a common unmarked grave.

Goliad is the site of the largest single loss of life in the fight for Texas Independence. The Goliad Massacre, accounted for twice the loss of life as at the Alamo, and inspired the battle cry: "Remember Goliad! Remember the Alamo!"

One of the darkest days in Texas history remains Palm Sunday, March 27, 1836, when Fannin and his men were massacred.

The human spirit remains restless in this kind of violent death and several ghost stories have been repeated over the years.

One security guard spent a terrifying night at the Presidio, when around midnight he heard the eerie wailing of infants. Unearthly cries echoed in the dark night, cries of pain and suffering. He said the cries came from several unmarked graves near the chapel.

People have reported sounds of a ghostly woman's choir wafting from the fortress.

A small, bare-footed friar wearing a black robe has been reported to wander the chapel grounds muttering in Latin. He appears, then disappears into a vapor like cloud.

A phantom dressed in a long, white, flowing-gown visits on dark nights. Perhaps she is looking for her groom who lost his life in the massacre.

There have been repeated reports of seeing lights late at night in the dark, closed chapel.

Also in the chapel, one tourist claimed to have seen a woman dressed in black, with a black veil over her face. The ghostly woman stood by the candles. There have been reports of mumbling noises, as if invisible people are praying.

The spirits of Goliad cry to us, moan to us, and remind us that when a human life meets a violent end, the spirit might not be able to rest.

The Lady of White Rock Lake
by Mitchel Whitington

Dallas, Texas

Ah, the good old days. I was sixteen years old, and riding in the passenger side of my friend's red Camaro with the windows down and the music from the eight-track player blaring. Life just doesn't get any better than that.

We'd been driving all over Texarkana, cruising the car lots looking for a particular automobile that my buddy had heard about. A friend of a friend of his had supposedly seen the car, a sleek, black Corvette with a price tag of only a thousand bucks. As the story was told, the owner of the car ran it off the road one night, and crashed down into a ravine. The poor soul died in the accident, and no one noticed the car for several weeks. Now, I'm trying not to get too graphic at this point, but let's just say that the decomposing body left an overly odorous presence in the Corvette.

The friend of a friend of my buddy had said that a local car dealer bought the vehicle at auction, and made all the necessary repairs, but there was one lingering problem: they couldn't get the smell out. New seats were installed, the carpet was replaced, the interior was completely re-worked – still, the scent of death would not leave the car.

And so we drove from one car lot to another that night, searching for the thousand-dollar 'Vette. My buddy and I never found it, though, and soon forgot about the legendary car. Not

157

before we told a few people, of course – the tale was much too interesting, and besides, a friend of a friend of my buddy had seen the Corvette, so it had to be true.

What does all this have to do with the Lady of White Rock Lake? Well, I'm getting there. Stay with me just a minute or two longer. You see, the Corvette story was only a faded memory for many years, until I picked up a book in the early 1980's by a man named Jan Harold Brunvand. He had assembled a book of widely circulated tales that are told as the truth, but in reality are just myths. On page 20 was the story of "The Death Car." Yep, my buddy and I had fallen prey to a phenomenon of the 20th century known as "urban legends," and it seems that the same story had spread from one coast to the other, with its roots in the fact that a friend of a friend had actually seen the automobile. Sometimes the type of car was different, or how the wreck occurred had changed a little, but the story was basically the same.

Now, on to White Rock Lake, and the famous spirit that walks its shores. It is a beautiful place – stroll along its walkways on any given day and you will encounter joggers, bicyclists, children playing, and folks like me who are just there for a little peace and quiet from the hectic pace of city life.

The lake was constructed in eastern Dallas in 1910 as a water supply for the city. The planners were interested in its beauty as well as its functionality, so tree-filled parks were built along the shores of the lake, and a winding road traced its circumference along with many pedestrian and bike trails. It is truly a magnificent place, and one that I love to visit.

As the sun begins to set over the lake, you can go to one of the lighted ball fields in the area to catch a softball game, or head down to the Bath House Cultural Center for a live performance or some other artistic exhibition. If you're just out for a leisurely evening drive, though, be careful about picking up hitchhikers – you may encounter the lake's phantom spirit.

One of the many trails around White Rock, where the ghostly lady takes her legendary stroll

The legend of the Lady of White Rock Lake has been in more newspaper stories, Texas ghost books, local Halloween television specials, and on Internet websites than any of the Dallas Cowboy football players. Okay, maybe that's a stretch, but the old girl does get around. According to the legend, if you were to have an encounter with the ghost it would go something like this:

You're driving around one of the lonelier parts of the lake on a particularly dark evening, when your headlights catch the figure of a young girl walking beside the road in a long, dripping wet party dress. Her hair is soaked, and she is carrying a pair of formal slippers as she trudges along in the grass on the shoulder of the road. She puts out her thumb as you approach, and since she definitely doesn't appear to be a threat, you stop and offer her a ride. The lovely young lady opens the rear door and climbs in to the back seat, then begins a tale of how her car was in an accident back down the road. The vehicle left the pavement and went into the lake, and she was thrown out into the water. The poor dear wasn't hurt, thankfully, but is concerned that her parents are worried about her being out so late. All she needs, the girl says with tear-glistening eyes, is a ride to her home. You nod sympathetically, and she gives you directions to one of the stately mansions looking out over the lake.

As you pull into the driveway that traverses the finely manicured lawn, you turn around to ask if you've found the correct house. Mysteriously, the girl has vanished! In the place where she was sitting, however, is a puddle of water on your seat cushion. You are understandably freaked out, and decide to knock on the door of the house to at least talk to the people there. An old, white-haired man opens the door slowly, and after hearing your tale, shakes his head and gives you a sad smile. He explains that his daughter was killed when the car that she was in went into the lake several decades ago, but every year on the anniversary of her death, she appears to some motorist who is kind enough to offer her a ride home.

That is how encounters with the Lady of White Rock Lake go. Unfortunately, it is impossible to find someone who actually picked up the girl. Or knocked on the door. Or had any encounter with a ghostly presence at the lake. When the story is told, however, it is always true – because it happened to a friend of a friend, just like my thousand-dollar Corvette story.

The title of the book by Brunvand that I mentioned earlier is, *The Vanishing Hitchhiker: American Urban Legends and Their Meanings.* As it turns out, most every city with a lake nearby has a similar story of a young, hitchhiking girl that vanishes in the car. Another variation features the poor thing knocking on the door of a home by the lake, asking to use the phone, then disappearing and leaving a puddle on the front porch. Yet another has her approaching young couples whose cars are parked out by the lake. Unfortunately the Lady of White Rock Lake, just like the Death Car that my buddy and I were looking for, is an urban legend.

Still, I didn't want to slight my readers, so I decided that the only prudent thing to do would be to give the ghostly gal a chance. I headed out for White Rock Lake, timing it so that the sun would just be setting when I arrived. As always, there were several people there, even though the crowd was thinning out because it was getting dark. I started out on the east side of the lake at Casa Linda shopping center, then went southwest on Garland Road and turned right to get to the lake. There are several roads into the park area at the south end of White Rock Lake, and I cruised them all, just in case the water-soaked girl was hanging around down there. No such luck.

I wasn't about to give up, though, so I hopped back on Garland Road for a bit, then left it again to follow Lawther Road up the western side of the lake. If there really is a ghost, she certainly wasn't looking for a ride on that particular night. I was pretty much alone.

On the north side I picked up Northwest Highway, and made a stop on Flagpole Hill. While researching the Lady of White Rock Lake story, I came upon a few additional notes about the area. The first was that Flagpole Hill was supposed to be a place where Satan Worshippers hung out, and that rocks would fly though the air at you, thrown by some invisible force. Another item that I'd heard about was that there is a bridge on Lawther where, if you stop as you cross over, your engine will die. I stopped on every bridge that I encountered, Lawther Road and otherwise, and my engine never died. On the other hand, maybe the guys at my local garage who keep my car in shape wield more power than the spirits on the bridge. One never knows.

Realizing that my trek would soon be over, I continued down Lawther along the east side of the lake, keeping my eyes peeled for anyone thumbing a lift. Alas, there was not a soul there, except for an occasional evening jogger with his reflective sneakers and headband.

I finally got on Buckner and headed back down to Casa Linda, a little disappointed. Not in the fact that I hadn't picked up the ghost – I never had any real expectations of finding the Lady of White Rock Lake. It just reminded me of that night back in Texarkana, driving home with my buddy, speculating how we'd get the smell out if we ever found the thousand-dollar 'Vette.

The Hanging of Chipita Rodriguez

by Vivian Kirkbride

San Patricio, Texas

The legendary Chipita Rodriguez is rumored to haunt Farm to Market Road 888 where the Nueces River separates San Patricio and Nueces counties. She was convicted and hanged by the neck from a mesquite tree for the axe murder of John Savage, a boarder at her traveler's inn. Surrounded by controversy, in fact, Chipita's tragic end took place on November 13, 1863, when she legally became the first woman to hang in Texas. Witnesses have seen Chipita appear as a phantom with a noose around her neck.

Chipita Rodriguez was a Tejano, born on Texas soil. It is believed that her father fled from Santa Anna and moved to San Patricio de Hibernia, Texas, in the 1830s. During the Texas Revolution, her father was killed. Orphaned, Chipita made her living by furnishing travelers with hot meals and a place to spread a bedroll on the front porch of her shack on the Aransas River.

In her twenties, Chipita married and had a son. Her husband, a cowboy, was gone for months at a time. When their son was four months old, her wandering husband kidnapped the infant and rode away. She never saw either of them again – until the night John Savage appeared.

162

She was likely in her 60s when the traveler John Savage came passing through. At the town saloon, Savage bragged about the $600 in gold he'd earned selling horses to the Union Army. He then rode out to Chipita's Inn to sleep off the night's drink.

On a muggy summer morning, after a morning walk, Chipita came home to the murder scene of the Cotton Road man. She saw a man standing over the dismembered body of John Savage. Her old eyes focused in on the man who stood over the body, holding the axe in his hand. Chipita thought she saw the face of her lost son as the killer ran off.

Panicked, she got her neighbor Juan Silvera to help wrap the body in a burlap bag and dump it in the Aransas River. The next morning two slaves pulled the sack out of the river. Two days later, Sheriff William Means had Chipita arrested.

It was presumed that Savage had been killed for the $600 in gold that he carried. When Savage's body was recovered along with the gold substantial doubt was raised about the motive for the crime, but Chipita and Juan Silvera, (who may have been her illegitimate son) were still charged with robbery and murder.

The two were indicted on circumstantial evidence and tried in San Patricio, where Chipita was kept in leg irons and chained to the wall in the courthouse.

Her only words of defense were, "Not guilty."

Most court records of that time were destroyed in the courthouse that burned under debatable circumstances on February 21, 1889. Few documents from the trial remain:

Minutes of the Distract Court of San Patricio County, P.111 states: We the jury, find the defendant Chipita Rodriguez guilty of murder in the first degree but on account of her old age and the circumstantial evidence against her do recommend her to the mercy of the court. (Signed) Owen Gaffney.

The jury asked for leniency but the judge called for death. Many claimed that Chipita was protecting her estranged, son,

Juan. Some say she was executed because she had been suspected of gathering information during the Civil War and framed for a political act.

By court order, on Friday the 13th, she was hanged by the neck until dead. Spectators claim to have heard her moan from the coffin, which was buried in an unmarked grave. Some say she was buried alive.

The first person to see her ghost was Juan Silvera. Sheriff Means reported seeing her on his way to church one Sunday evening.

In 1985 the Texas legislature absolved Chipita Rodriguez of murder, due to irregularities in the proceedings. But she still haunts the area, particularly whenever another woman is sentenced to be executed. Anyone from that region knows that if you see the wraith with a noose around her neck, it's the phantom of Chipita Rodriguez.

Entertaining Angels Unaware

by Ann Greenfield

Alice, Texas

Juan stopped on U.S. Highway 44 outside of Agua Dulce, Texas. "Sister, do you need a ride?" he asked.

"Yes, thank you. How far are you going?" the nun asked.

"I'm going to the Works Progress Administration office in Alice," Juan said. He held the car door open for the nun.

"Splendid. I'm going to Alice to do some sewing for the WPA as well," said the sister. She climbed in the front seat, adjusted her black habit, and folded her hands in her lap.

"Do you have any children in the armed services?" asked the sister.

"I have a son in the navy, and my nephew was killed at Pearl Harbor," said Juan.

"I'm sorry for your loss. Rest assured Juan, your nephew did not die in vain. Freedom is the right of every person. This war will be over by the end of 1942, until then, I'll keep the safety of your son in my prayers," said the sister.

"Thank you Sister." Juan smiled sadly and blinked the tears from his eyes. They continued down the road in silence.

"We're here." Juan parked the car near the WPA sewing center just off of Main Street across the street from a garage, and quickly walked around to the passenger side and opened the door for the nun. "I'll be returning to Corpus in the late afternoon. Can I give you a ride back to Agua Dulce?"

"That would be lovely." The nun took Juan's hand and clasped it between both of hers. She looked into his brown eyes and smiled. "Bless you and yours, my son," she said and made the sign of the cross.

Juan returned that afternoon, but found the sister gone. In his search one of the women working at the WPA sewing center approached him, "Who are you looking for?"

Juan held his hat in both hands and fiddled with the worn brim. "Sister Hope, I dropped her off this morning," said Juan.

"Sir, no nuns volunteer at this WPA sewing center," informed the woman.

"That's strange. Is there a convent or church near by?" asked Juan.

"Go two blocks, turn left, go another block and a half and St. Joseph's and the Dominican Sisters are at the end of the dirt road. You can't miss it," said the woman.

"Thank you for your help." Juan gave a slight bow. He then placed his hat on his head, and walked out the door.

"Good afternoon Sister," said Juan knocking on the rectory door. The sister at St. Joseph's looked up from her cluttered desk. "Please come in." She removed her glasses, and motioned for Juan to enter the office. "How can I help you?" asked the Mother Superior.

"I'm looking for one of your Sisters. At least I think she is. She was going to ride back to Agua Dulce with me this afternoon," said Juan.

"What is her name?" asked the Mother Superior.

"Sister Hope," said Juan.

Mother Superior took both of Juan's hands in between her own, her voice a soft whisper, "My son, she's been dead, now... for eight years."

* * * * *

Corporal Lopez leaned out of the passenger window of a Chevrolet Bel Air as it slowed to a stop on U.S. Highway 77, just outside Sinton. "Sister, can we help you?"

"If you young men are going to Corpus Christi, I could use a ride?" requested the nun.

He opened his door, stepped out and blew smoke from his nostrils. "I'm Corporal Lopez. We're at your service, Sister." He dropped his cigarette butt on the ground, covered it with the toe of his boot and twisted his foot. He pushed the front seat forward and climbed into the back.

"And I'm Corporal Martinez," said a broad-shouldered man as he walked around to the passenger side. He put out his hand and helped the nun get into the front seat. He waited until she gathered her black habit inside the car then slammed the door.

"Are you boys on leave," asked the nun?

"Yes Sister, we're home for a week," said Martinez.

"Where are you boys stationed," asked the nun?

"Da Nang," said Lopez. He lit another cigarette.

"The war will be over soon," promised the nun.

"I'll drink to that," said Lopez. He opened a can of beer and raised it in a toast.

Martinez gave him a dirty look. Lopez shrugged.

"Please drop me off at the cemetery," said the nun as they reached the outskirts of Corpus Christi. Martinez stopped the car in front of the gates. He ran around to the passenger side and opened the door for the nun.

"Would you like for us to wait?" asked Corporal Martinez.

"No thank you," said the nun.

"Do you need a ride back to Sinton?" asked Corporal Lopez. He climbed out of the back seat and stood beside Martinez.

The nun shook her head no.

"Is there anything else we can do for you? Pick you up later? Call someone to come and get you?" asked Corporal Martinez.

"Well, there is one thing. You can give this note to the padre at Sinton." The nun pulled a worn post card from the folds of her skirt and handed it to him.

Corporal Lopez shoved Martinez' hand and reached for the postcard, he clasped the nun's wrist with his free hand. "Sister, *por favor*... a *bendición*, will you give us a blessing?"

She extended her hand to include Corporal Martinez. He stuffed the postcard into his pocket and grasped her hand. The nun bowed her head and said a silent prayer. She released their hands and made the sign of the cross in front of each soldier, "Bless you my son. Go with God." She turned and walked through the cemetery gate.

The two soldiers went to the church in Sinton, Texas and found the priest in his office.

"Hello, Padre. I'm Corporal Lopez." He shook hands with the priest. "And this is my buddy Corporal Martinez."

They waited while the priest read the postcard.

Hi Soldier! We want you to know that you are missed very much and that we are with you every hour of the day. You have a big job to do for the world and for the church. May you find strength and guidance in the words of God.

The old priest peered at them over the tops of his glasses. He flipped the card over and glanced at the back. It was blank. Then he showed the soldiers the card holding it between both hands.

"This is a World War II Victory greeting card," said the priest.

They shrugged.

The priest continued, "From 1942..."

The two soldiers looked at each other and back at the priest.

"Is something wrong?" asked Lopez.

"This is 1967!" The priest searched the faces of the soldiers. Corporal Lopez shifted his weight and popped a cigarette in his mouth. The priest wagged his finger. Lopez removed the cigarette and placed it behind his ear.

"Where did you get this card?" demanded the priest.

"The nun was walking along the road and we offered her a ride. We dropped her at the cemetery, per her request. We figured she was visiting a grave. She asked us to give you the postcard. And that's it," explained Martinez.

"What's her name?" asked the priest.

"We didn't ask her name, Padre," offered Martinez shifting his weight.

"We haven't had any nuns at this church in many years, but I do have pictures. Would you recognize her?" asked the priest.

Both Lopez and Martinez nodded.

The priest rummaged through book shelves and found a brown leather album. The edges were worn and the pages were yellowed. He blew dust from the front of the book and began flipping pages. He stopped at a group picture and handed the album to Martinez. Lopez looked over his shoulder.

They searched over the group. Lopez pointed to one of the nuns, "It's this one, Padre."

The padre put on his spectacles, then took the album and studied the photo.

"Oh no," the priest gasped, "It can't be... Not again!"

"Who is she?" asked Martinez steadying the priest by the elbow.

The priest closed the photo album, placed it back on the shelf, removed his glasses and rubbed his eyes. "I'm sorry to tell you boys, but Sister Hope has been dead for many years."

* * * * *

At a scheduled stop on U.S. Highway 59 in Goliad a small woman with blue eyes appeared beside the bus. A warm Texas breeze allowed her scuffed lace-up shoes to peek out from beneath her billowing black habit. The paleness of her face was accentuated by her black shoulder-length veil.

"Let me help you with your bags, Sister?" said the bus driver. He loaded the bags and helped the nun onto the bus. Her hands were shriveled and boney compared with the smoothness of her face.

"Thank you, Jorge," said the nun in a soft quiet voice. She sat in the aisle seat two rows behind the driver.

Jorge Gonzalez wondered how the nun knew his name. Then he remembered he was wearing a nametag. He closed the bus doors, pulled onto U.S. Highway 59 bound for Laredo and smiled at the nun in the rear view mirror. Her smile was radiant.

Jorge felt calm, a sense of peace. Was it the nun's presence?

A soldier flicked his cigarette out of the open window. Jorge kept most of the windows opened when he traveled through this hot south Texas region known as the Rio Grande Valley. He didn't want to be roasted alive inside the traveling metal oven. The smell of dust from the parched ranch land blew into the bus with each gust of wind.

Several minutes passed, and Jorge watched the nun cross the aisle to a man sitting in the first row. The gaunt man had a sad, distant look in his brown eyes. She spent several minutes listening to the uniformed man. Jorge couldn't hear all of their conversation over the noise of the road, but he did hear them talk about the war in Iraq and how awful it was.

One thing in particular caught Jorge's ear. The nun told the soldier that the war would be over by the end of the year. *Maybe nuns had a direct link to God and knew something no one else did.* He hoped she was right. The United States had entered the war on terror after the bombing of the Twin Towers in New York.

Jorge was jarred out of his own thoughts by laughter. He glanced toward the sound and observed a small child setting next to his mother. The child giggled with each peek-a-boo from the old soldier behind him. The nun patted the child's head and made the sign of the cross. When she finished the blessing she said, "You'll make a find soldier one day."

The nun turned her attention to the young soldier who sat across the isle. The sister pulled a black and red rosary out of her pocket. She wrapped it around her left hand and clasped the metal cross between her thumb and forefinger.

The tires made a thudding sound and the bus trembled.

The nun stood steadfast and still. She seemed unaffected by the rocking motion of the bus over potholes in the road. She touched the young man's shoulder with the tips of her right hand. The tension drained from his body and his whole demeanor relaxed. She whispered something in his ear. They both bowed their heads. Then the nun made the sign of the cross directly in front of the soldier's face and kissed the rosary cross.

"Bless you, my son," she patted the corporal on the back. The young corporal slumped down as best he could and shut his eyes. As he slept, all tension vanished.

About mid-way down the aisle the nun crossed back to the left side of the bus. She changed the rosary to the right hand and slipped into the seat next to a soldier with a bandage around his head. They sat in silence. After a long while the nun made the sign of the cross. The wounded soldier continued to sleep.

She continued down the aisle stopping at each uniformed service man. She repeated the procedure visiting and blessing each soldier. Afterwards, the soldiers were calm and had a peaceful glow on their faces.

Later that afternoon one of the soldiers came to the front of the bus, "Where is the sister?"

"She walked to the back of the bus and hasn't returned to her seat," said the bus driver. He looked in the rear view mirror for the nun.

"She's not in the back. I just came from there. I didn't see her when I walked up here," said the soldier.

"She's probably talking to one of the men," reassured the bus driver.

"No, she's not anywhere on the bus," insisted the private.

"Where could she go?" said the driver. "We haven't stopped the bus since she got on, so she has to be here."

"Could she have fallen out of the window?" the soldier persisted.

"No, she couldn't!"

"Well, she's not here and no one has seen her!" claimed the private and stomped back to his seat.

Finally the bus driver stopped the bus. He walked down the aisle checking the passengers carefully and beneath each seat. No nun! Jorge walked around the outside of the bus. He searched under the bus and looked behind each tire. He opened the baggage compartment. The nun's bags were gone. She had vanished.

* * * * *

Was there a nun who traveled the roads in south Texas in 1942 comforting, blessing and giving hope to soldiers – soldiers who fought for our freedom? Could she be blessing soldiers today?

Be careful who you pick up along the south Texas highways! You never know if you may be entertaining angels unaware.

The Legend of *El Muerto*, "The Dead One"

by Dede Harper

Ben Bolt, Texas

Tall tales and tall Texans... the State of Texas has had its fair share of both. From all encounters, the legend of El Muerto has a bit of the above and more. Two larger-than-life Texans, Big Foot Wallace and Creed Taylor, took the law into their own hands to send a message to horse thieves in the region. At the crux of this tale is a headless horseman seen wandering the counties where these two legendary men thrived. Such sightings have occurred over a two hundred and fifty mile radius in the last two centuries.

The area in question spans from Creed's ranch off of Farm to Market Road 479, about nineteen miles east of present day Junction in Kimble County in Southwest Texas, to several counties down and over around Ben Bolt, Texas. Ben Bolt is a small city in Jim Wells County, located seven or so counties southeast of Creed Taylor's Ranch. It is in this area around Ben Bolt, located off of U.S. Highway 281, just south of Alice, that El Muerto was supposedly laid to rest, and where he haunts the area. Further over, and especially on dark moonless nights, El Muerto has been seen galloping in the distance in the counties of the West Texas brush country. He's been seen as far west as

173

Uvalde, around Farm to Market Road 140 near the historic cavalry post of Fort Inge.

Some might call the legend of El Muerto a grizzly tale full of unnecessary violence; that's why the headless horseman haunts the highways today. Regardless, it's the presence of these two Texas Rangers in the tale that thrusts it into legendary status.

William Alexander Anderson Wallace, a direct descendent of William Wallace of old Scotland, found his way from Virginia to Texas back in 1837. A big man who stood six foot-two inches, Captain Wallace weighed around two hundred and forty pounds, with no extra fat on his body. He left a serious impression and most men did not take him lightly. Being a large man who wore moccasins, his identity was once confused with an Indian with fourteen inch long feet and thus, the nickname "Big Foot" stuck.

Big Foot Wallace came to Texas originally to exact revenge on the Mexican army who took his brother Sam's life at the infamous massacre at Goliad during the Texas Revolution. He participated in some of the raids to release prisoners held by Santa Anna, most notably the failed Mier Expedition, and ended up spending time in a well-known Mexican prison called Perote prison. Later, he became a renowned Indian fighter. When Sam Houston asked Captain John Coffee Hays to form the Texas Rangers, Hays said any man who wanted to join needed to "have courage, be of good character, be a good rider, be a good shot and have a horse worth $100." When Big Foot Wallace joined the rangers, some historians say the outfit became the best set of Indian fighters ever formed, and it just so happens this group included another legendary Texan, Creed Taylor.

Creed Taylor, like Big Foot Wallace, was known for getting his hands bloodied. He first came to notoriety when at the age of fifteen, he helped defend the "Come and Take it" Gonzales cannon from the Mexican army. After the Alamo fell, he led his family to safety in the Runaway Scrape, then came back and fought at the battle of San Jacinto, helping to defeat Santa Anna's army and thereby establishing the Republic of Texas. In 1841 he joined the Texas Rangers and fought the Comanche most notably at Plum Creek and Bandera Pass. He also enlisted as a Texas Mounted Ranger and fought in the Mexican War in 1846, and then later fought on the side of the Confederacy in the Civil War. Creed Taylor is also known for surviving the bloodiest feud in the state of Texas, in which one that his own family played a major part, the Taylor-Sutton feud.

It was with what had to be shear bad luck or remarkable stupidity that a horse thief by the name of Vidal embarked on a mission to steal some of Creed Taylor's cows and prized wild mustangs from his ranch along the Nueces River. This area bordered what was then referred to as "No Man's Land." No Man's Land extended south from Taylor's ranch on the Nueces to the Rio Grande River. And it was a lawless territory. Bands of renegade Indians and nefarious outlaws roamed the area, raiding the ranches that butted up to this scruffy terrain. Because Creed Taylor's ranch bordered this area, his ranch felt the brunt of many of these attacks.

One version of the El Muerto legend begins with Vidal and his gang of lowly horse thieves operating in and around No Man's Land for some time before being caught. The thieves had the sad misfortune of stealing cattle from the Flores family (for which Floresville is named) and from the Taylor ranch while Creed Taylor was in residence. According to one version of the legend, Creed Taylor and members of the Flores family ran into Big Foot Wallace as they set out to track the thieves. Wallace threw in with them, and with these two great trackers in pursuit, they came upon the thieves shortly thereafter. (Still another version of the legend has Creed Taylor and the Flores men going after Vidal without Big Foot in their company.)

Tired of being the victims of such raids, Creed Taylor and the other men decided to deal harshly with the thieves. They cut off the head of the man called Vidal in order to make a statement and hopefully deter anyone else from stealing their cattle. They took the dead man's body and slung it upon the back of a wild mustang, tied it to the saddle, then propped the body up with a pole. The unbroken mustang ran all over the countryside, bucking like crazy while the headless body remarkably stayed in the saddle, frightening everyone it encountered. The horse took to the hills scaring many cowboys and Indians as it bucked its way around the territory. Thus, the name "El Muerto," or The Dead One, began to be used referring to the mustang and its hair-raising burden.

In a completely different version of the story, one told by Creed to J. Warren Hunter, a historian, and later appearing in Hunter's 1898 manuscript, "The Life of Creed Taylor," it is Big Foot Wallace who decides to extort the punishment along with a ranger friend by the name of John McPeters. As part of the Texas Rangers, Wallace and McPeters tracked renegade Indians as well as other outlaws, including horse thieves. Supposedly Vidal's real name was Vuavis, a Mexican lieutenant turned bandit whom Wallace had encountered during his battle days of the Texas Revolution. Big Foot not only beheaded the man and saddled the wild mustang with the body but he also tied the decapitated head to the pommel of the saddle along with a sombrero and set it upon the horse, so it could roam the countryside as a warning to other horse thieves in the area.

The mustang carrying its burden of El Muerto was credited with all kinds of calamities. Some witnesses reported seeing flames shooting out of its nose. By this time, the decapitated head had darkened and become badly shrunken by the fiery Texas sun. By the time men caught up to the mustang, the body had been peppered with bullets and pierced with arrows by those it had frightened along the way.

The headless horseman was finally caught by some cowboys and buried about two miles west of Ben Bolt. And thus, the haunting began, for in such a disturbing and gruesome death, one does not forget so easily. Others say the punishment fit the crime for stealing cattle was a hanging offense back then, and the headless horseman seen along Farm to Market Road 140 and U.S. Highway 281 serves as a reminder to leave another man's bread and butter alone.

Not so surprisingly, these legendary Texans accomplished what they'd set out to do: the message of El Muerto lives on, even if they do not.

Vindication, But at What Cost?

by Tammy Petty Conrad

Alice, Texas

I have heard startled drivers whisper about a woman dressed in black who sometimes appears near the Farm to Market Road 141 underpass at U.S. Highway 281, between Premont and Ben Bolt, near Alice. Out of kindness, some have even picked her up, only to discover that upon reaching their destination, there is no passenger.

The woman's story is as sad as she appears to be on the side of the road. Locals know her to be Dona Leonora Rodriguez de Ramos. As a young woman she was brought from Mexico to be the wife of a great landowner in Falfurrias in the 1700s. It is as familiar a tale as the stories of today's rich and famous. She was young and beautiful. He was handsome and wealthy. But her new husband, Don Raul Ramos, was a man of great anger and it seems he let his passion overwhelm him, which brought a great tragedy to the area.

Shortly after the couple married, he was called to Spain to attend to urgent business. When he returned after over six months, he found his new wife pregnant, which brought him great joy, that is, until rumors reached him of his wife's wandering ways. The story goes that the gossip was started by a local woman who had expected to be Mrs. Ramos. I can only wonder if this woman was later tortured by the outcome of her maliciousness. Needless to say, her story goes untold.

Ramos gave his bride no opportunity to prove her faithfulness, but instead sent her away with two of his ranch hands with very precise instructions. According to the household servants, she was dressed in black and forcefully driven from her hacienda a day's ride north. Interestingly, he may have feared coming to his senses, because at the same time, he headed south.

This makes for a great story, one to be told on a dark night around a campfire, of an innocent woman vowing to her wardens that one day she would show them she was telling the truth. According to the legend, she promised before her death that they would see her again in their lifetime and then they would know she was innocent.

I envision this distraught woman bouncing along in her carriage with armed guards on either side of her realizing that there was no chance of escape. I imagine after pleading for hours to be released, that instead of becoming hopeless, she became resolved to meet her demise with dignity. How strong she must have been to meet the eyes of her killers with her vow to return. Could she have imagined that at the very same moment the noose was tightened around her delicate neck that her husband was blowing his brains out because of his evil deed?

The first sighting was on the anniversary of her death. A family stopped their wagon to help a woman near the very spot La Dona was supposedly buried. They didn't know who she was, but she shared the story of the death of a wrongly accused woman. Of course by the time they reached a town, she was gone. And the legend began. Sightings continued throughout the years.

Today witnesses include drivers who think they hit someone, but never find a body. There are others who see a woman dressed in old fashioned black clothing one minute on the side of the road and then when they glance back, there is nothing. Locals know her story and they share it with their children so that the legend of the woman wrongly accused will live on.

I wonder when Leonora will feel she can rest with her baby and not wander the desolate area of her demise. If that ever happens there will no longer be a beautiful vision to distract drivers, but only a haunting story that will live in their memory as a reminder of the power of anger and the destruction caused by rumors.

The Girl in the Pink Dress
by MaryBeth Gradziel

Benavides, Texas

Many a wistful tale is told of a beautiful, young women standing alone by the roadside – a rural highway somewhere that is usually in the south.

The location depends on the storyteller. Here in Texas, more often than not, the young lady is standing on State Highway 339 and State Highway 359 toward Benavides in far South Texas. She is said to be wearing a slightly out-of-fashion pink dress, and her name is "Maria."

On a Saturday night in 1950, Manuel had been working hard all day at his second job, the one that made it possible for him to buy a new red-and-white Chevy half-ton truck, which he was extremely proud of. On a particular Saturday night, his girlfriend, Margarita, complained that he would rather spend his money on the truck than on her, and had flounced off in a huff.

She was right, of course, and he was more relieved than upset at her leaving. He wasn't sure if he'd even ask her to dance if she showed up at the Fiesta in Benavides. They'd planned to attend the event together before she'd stormed off.

Margarita had hinted more than once that she was impatiently expecting a diamond ring from him – the bigger the better. When he bought the truck instead, Margarita chastised him loudly, saying what an idiot he was, and that he obviously was not the kind of man she'd thought. She felt that deserved so much better and wasn't going to waste her time with such a loser.

When the verbal barrage stopped, Manuel looked up from *Car & Driver* magazine he was reading just in time to see the door slam behind her. He liked the sudden quiet, and didn't bothered to call her all week.

It was soon Saturday night again. He showered, splashed on after-shave, and dressed carefully in his new narrow-cut pants and light yellow shirt that was cut just right to show off his bulging biceps. He wore the bolo that had been his father's, and slipped into his dress boots. Manuel slung his new leather jacket over his shoulder and caught himself with a backward glance at the mirror. He was looking good – girls, watch out!

Fortunately he was doing less than the speed limit when his headlights caught the shape of a young woman standing on the side of the road on the way to Benavides. He wasn't able to slow down fast enough the first time he saw her, so he had to turn around and go back, looping over to where she stood.

"Good Evening," he said politely. "Are you all right? My name is Manuel. Can I help you?" He saw that she was exceptionally pretty, with long, curly lashes framing liquid, chocolate eyes that danced with a hint of mischief.

"Hello, Manuel," she answered. "My name is Maria." She giggled and blushed a little because he looked at her so intently. "Yes, you can help me. I am lonely and I no longer know anyone around here. I want to have fun. I want to go dancing. Will you take me dancing?"

"Yes! I am on my way to the Fiesta in Benavides. There will be great music for dancing!" Manuel jumped out of his truck, ran over to the passenger side, opened the door and helped Maria into his truck. She was light as a feather, and so pretty. He could not believe his good luck.

On the way to the fiesta they chatted. Manuel asked Maria why he had not seen her at the other dances. After all, he never missed a fiesta, and loved to dance.

She answered shyly that she had been away for ten years and had not been to a fiesta in that long. She stared out the window and seemed so sad that Manuel could not bear it. But he soon had her laughing as her told her about the antics of two young kittens he had taken in. They liked to play-fight with each other and would leap up in the air to put on a show for him each evening after he came home from work.

Before they knew it, Manuel and Maria were at the fiesta, holding hands and walking together to the dance floor as if they had always known each other.

They danced, danced, and danced some more. Manuel had never before met a woman who loved to dance as much as he did. She didn't seem to know the latest dances at first, but she caught on quickly. And when the band played polkas, she was phenomenal. He had never seen anyone dance the polka the way Maria danced. Around and around the dance floor they went, Maria spinning endlessly. The skirt of her slightly old-fashioned pink dress twirled around her shapely legs. Manuel could not take his eyes off her. Time flew by. Suddenly it was midnight and the band played the last dance.

As they stepped outside and walked to his truck in the cool night air, Manuel saw that Maria was shivering in her delicate pink dress. As any gentleman would, he wrapped his jacket around her slender shoulders. They did not talk much on the way back. Maria snuggled against Manuel, with her head against his chest. When they approached the place where he had picked her up, she suddenly slid quickly toward the passenger door and insisted he leave her off by the side of the road, right where he had found her. No matter what Manuel said, he could not change her mind.

"At least take my jacket with you to keep you warm." He gave in, thinking that he would return tomorrow to reclaim his jacket and take her out to dinner. As he drove off, he tried to watch her silhouette to see which way she went, but she seemed to disappear almost instantly.

The next morning, Manuel could hardly wait to drive back to where he had found Maria. Slightly further down the road was an old farmhouse – the only building he could see. Surely that had to be Maria's house. Politely, he knocked on the door, hoping that Maria would be the one to open it. At first there was no response, so he knocked more loudly. The door opened and an older woman with sad brown eyes stepped out on to the porch.

"Yes?" she asked quizzically, with lifted eyebrows.

"I have come to see Maria," Manuel explained.

But the woman drew back in the doorway, startled and her eyes started to fill with tears.

"Is Maria not here?" Manuel asked.

"No. No, "the woman answered. "You are too cruel. You must know that my Maria died ten years ago!"

"No!" Manuel answered, shocked. "That cannot be! I met her only last night. We danced and danced. But she would not let me bring here all the way home. She insisted I leave her on the side of the road, over there." He pointed to where he had met Maria.

The woman stared at him, then grabbed his hand and pulled him across the road to the spot he had indicated. As they ran, Manuel told her again how beautiful Maria had been in her old-fashioned pink dress and how well she danced, especially the polka. He described the dress in detail.

"Si," the woman said. "That was my Maria's favorite dress. That was the dress we buried her in after the accident." She pulled Manuel to a small cemetery on the side of the road. "Look! This is our family cemetery, and here is her tombstone."

It read: *Maria Lozano, 1920-1940*

The woman continued. "She died ten years ago. But, look!" She pointed to the ground, where across the grave, folded neatly, was Manuel's leather jacket.

The story has been repeated through the years – many people believe the tale of Manuel and his night of passion with Maria, while others regale it to the world of urban legends. No matter what the truth is, the story of the girl in the pink dress continues to be told.

The Visitant
by Hernan Moreno-Hinojosa

Bruni, Texas

I first heard of the mysterious apparition from Jesse Guerra
back in the late eighties. Jesse owned the G&G Convenience
store in Bruni. The old country store, made of cinder blocks,
was situated on a big dirt lot just off Texas State Highway 359
that runs from Hebbronville into Laredo. Jesse sold gasoline,
groceries, beer and just about anything a person might need if
he didn't care to drive fifty miles west to Laredo.

Early that morning I pulled up to the gas pumps and began
to fuel my van. I had open credit with the G & G and it was
customary for a person with an account to just pump his gas
and then go inside to sign for it.

I'd just started to fuel when I noticed Jesse hurry out of his
store and walk rapidly toward me. He wore a somber
expression and I wonder I had exceeded my credit limit for the
month. But, Jesse greeted me with his customary "morning"
but went on to relate how something unseemly had occurred to
our mutual friend Julio Perez around midnight.

"This happened today?" I asked.

"Yeah, this morning," Jesse said. "Julio was coming into
town late from work in Hebbronville when he noticed a woman
on the side of the road hitching a ride. It was around midnight
and he figured that it had to be a local person whose car had
broken down, and so he stopped."

Like in all small towns everyone is acquainted and they especially take note of what everyone drives, so it would have been unconscionable for a fellow resident not to stop and help out another person stranded on the road. If Julio failed to stop, the next day he would be the talk of the town, *Julio just drove by last night, never bothering to try and help old so-and-so who was stranded on the highway!*

"When the woman was close enough, Julio lowered his window to see who she was. You know that he never got the power windows fixed on that old diesel Suburban he drives," Jesse said.

I nodded. Julio loved that Suburban SUV which he bought new, way back when. Now the power windows were molasses-slow opening and closing. Nonetheless, diesels hold up better than regular cars and so he'd never replaced it.

"Well sir," Jesse said solemnly, "those windows are tinted dark, and when Julio finally got that window down far enough to afford a good look, he did the only thing he could do. He dropped that old Suburban into drive and burned the rubber off the tires gettin' the hell outta there!"

I had trouble visualizing that tired old diesel engine spinning its rear tires hard enough to burn rubber. In my head was an image of Julio's old tan and brown suburban lumbering away in the dead of night. I stared incredulously at Jesse whose expression never changed.

"Now why would Julio do that?"

"Well guy," Jesse gesticulated with his hands, "he did what he had to do."

"What do you mean?" I was more puzzled than ever since this convoluted conversation began.

"Imagine Julio's astonishment," Jesse clarified, "to see standing there in the naked moonlight, a horrible man with a bald pate, full beard and mustache wearing a sleek black sequined gown slit to *there* and red high-heel woman's shoes!"

187

Now it was my turn to stare wide-eyed at Jesse. "Who was he?"

Jesse shook his head slowly. "We haven't figured that one out yet."

I took a moment to ponder Jesse's strange story and decided to just talk to Julio about it later. With more important things on my mind I took leave of Jesse with the usual *'til later* and soon forgot his strange story.

* * * * *

It was some three days later that I again heard the strange story again. This time at where I worked at the El Mesquite Uranium Plant located off State Highway 359, the very highway where Julio had his odd encounter. The cleaning lady who reports to work at midnight at the uranium plant suffered a near-fatal heart attack after coming face-to-face with the apparition now known regionally as *The Visitant*. I'm not sure who coined the term for the strange night caller but Ruben Cantu was telling the story when I arrived. Ruben is called *Twitty* by his close friends and so I asked, "Hey Twitty, what visitant?"

"You know how the cleaning lady drives in each night from Hebbronville?"

"Mrs. Dooley?"

Twitty nodded.

"Well last night," Twitty said. "She didn't quite make it."

"What–" I interrupted concerned that something bad might have happened to such a nice, harmless God-fearing older lady.

"Last night," Twitty continued, "she started out for work as usual, arriving at the front gate a few minutes before midnight. She buzzed the security guard to let her in, when something occurred."

The uranium plant is located five or six miles north of the highway. A visitor buzzes the security guard on the intercom, and states his business. Once recognized, the security guard throws a toggle switch and the sixteen-foot long chain-link gate will begin to open very slowly. When the gate is completely open the visitor has a few seconds to clear the entrance before the gate automatically closes. That gate always closes quicker than it opens and has been known to strike some cars before they can clear the entrance.

"Anyway, as Mrs. Dooley waited on the gate to finish opening a young lady seemed to appear by the driver's side door. She wore a long black dress with shiners all over it, cut on the side of the leg real sexy–"

Irritated that he was taking so long with his story, I interrupted, "A sequined gown?"

Twitty thought about this for a second, snapped his fingers loudly and stated, "Yeah, I think that's what Mrs. Dooley said, *a sequined gown*. Anyway, she was just wondering where this young lady could have come from since she hadn't seen any cars nearby. It isn't likely that anyone could have walked to the plant entrance as it is right in the middle of nowhere."

Now where have I heard this story before?

"Mrs. Dooley couldn't see the girl's face yet because she towered over her car..."

Twitty was a good storyteller and we all hung on his every word.

"Well just imagine Mrs. Dooley's fright, salt-of-the-earth person that she is, when the apparition lowered her countenance to the driver's side window with both hands still gripping the roof of her car really up front and personal! That was no girl standing there all dressed up in a fancy gown like Cinderella fixing to go to the ball! It was a bald-headed man with full-beard and mustache, and he just started cussing up a blue streak when Mrs. Dooley proceeded to drive off! Apparently he was mad because Mrs. Dooley wouldn't give him a ride!

189

"The gate hadn't even finished opening when Mrs. Dooley drove through it. The gate slapped the entire passenger side of her car she was in such a hurry. Mrs. Dooley said she'd never heard such horrible language in her entire life. She was hyperventilating and we were afraid that she was having a heart attack. Anyway we called for the air ambulance out of Falfurrias to transport her to the Medical Center in Corpus Christi."

All I could say was, "Unbelievable!" I knew we had an elected deputy constable who could never be found, and with the true police jurisdiction being 50 miles west in Laredo we never did have adequate police coverage. I asked anyway, "Did anyone investigate?"

"Sure," Twitty added enthusiastically, "Robert Muñoz, the shift supervisor called the Border Patrol."

"The Border Patrol? I know that Border Patrolmen pickup illegal aliens but I had no idea that they searched for spooks."

Twitty sounded a little sheepish when he explained. "We couldn't be completely sure that we weren't dealing with an illegal alien, so we called the Border Patrol."

Around here Mexican citizens escaping to the U.S. get blamed for everything. Someone's laundry disappears from the clothesline and illegal aliens get the blame. Some kid's bike disappears from the front porch and they again got blamed. I'm surprised that junior high kids aren't telling their teachers that an illegal alien stole their homework.

"So," Twitty continued, "Robert and a couple of agents from the Border Patrol met up by the front gate and proceeded to look around. Nothing! Which is why we were thinking that it might have been one of those *aparecidos* old timers talk about. You know, a *visitant*, a ghost sent to haunt people for their misdeeds."

"Misdeeds? What misdeeds could poor Mrs. Dooley be guilty of?" I asked.

Twitty looked down. "Well, you know, she was just probably at the wrong place at the wrong time."

* * * * *

The people of South Texas are not an uncommonly fearful lot. To be sure my friend Julio's reaction was odd, as was Mrs. Dooley's, the cleaning lady. That morning when I left the G & G Store after listening to Jesse's enthralling account of Julio's misadventure with the mysterious apparition I too had a close encounter with The Visitant. As I drove toward Hebbronville, Texas close to the entrance to the uranium plant where we worked, I saw a man of short and stocky stature. He was bald, and he wore white coveralls. He sat on the ground with his knees pulled up to his chest. His back rested against a road reflector and he appeared quite destitute. I could see that he was drinking something out of a can and so I did not react immediately. This was during the middle of summer and the daily temperature was already approaching over a hundred. The dual air conditioning on my van labored on max against the relentless heat of day. I thought to myself, *if someone doesn't give that poor guy a ride soon he'll suffer heat stroke.* The man sat on the westbound side of the road as I traveled east and so I made a mental note to look for him on my return trip.

Some forty-five minutes later I was going back and had completely forgotten about the stranded man until I saw him in the same place. Since I was traveling at highway speed I came to a stop some distance from where he rested. In my right outboard mirror I observed the individual in white overalls stare intently at my van, then rise reluctantly and start uncertainly toward me. When he reached the passenger side door he hesitated as if appraising the situation. I motioned for him to open the door and climb in. As the door opened I got quite a start when I heard someone say in a voice that was not a

191

man's voice, "Mister are you *really* going to give me a ride or are you just fooling like all the others?"

There were two things I realized immediately – and I am choosing my words very carefully so please listen. One: If this encounter were not *sanctified* by the holy light of day, I would have immediately reacted quite like my friend, fleeing immediately and leave the hitchhiker to fend for himself. Two: With a chill I came to the realization that the person soliciting the ride was not a man at all; no sir, he was a woman! Her face was so dirty with road grim that at night the shadow would certainly appear to be a full beard and mustache. She wore her hair in an atrocious style, cut very close to the scalp, quite common further west where it is known as the *burr cut*.

Recovering from my surprise I replied, "Of course I'm gonna give you a ride Miss! Where are you going?"

"Just the next town," she said. "You know, people here just aren't worth a damn!"

"Now what makes you say that Miss?"

She managed a small smile and politely extended her right hand saying, "I'm sorry. Please allow me to introduce myself. I am Geraldine Lowe. Please call me 'Geri.'" Then she added somberly, "People here pull over making you think you're going to get a ride. After you walk all the way up to their car they just peel out leaving you standing there in the dust!"

I took her hand remembering what a mad monk (or ex-nun?) had once told me about giving out your *real* name, *Your name gives power over you to others* and so at a pinch I coined a name, "Rupert Garcia here, *enchanté* Miss Geri!"

Flying westward toward Bruni, Geri asked, "Do people here always drive this fast?"

"Wide open space Miss. No highway patrol so we crowd the speed limit a little bit."

"Oh." She seemed unsure; indeed the explanation sounded lame even to me. Now she reached into her tote bag she carried and asked, "Do mind if I have a beer?"

I shook my head as she retrieved a *Miller Lite* beer and offered it to me. Hmm, a black sequined gown, and red high heel pumps could easily be stored in that tote bag along with what was left of a six-pack of beer!

"I can't believe that no one would give you a ride."

"I've been here for three days and nights. Nobody gave me a ride."

"I can tell you're not from here. So tell me Geri, how did you become stranded here?"

"You're right. I'm from New Mexico. There's no work there and so I hitched a ride with a local man who assured me there was a lot of work in South Texas. Then he dropped me off by that gate and told me to ask someone for work."

"The uranium plants have a hiring freeze, so I guess you were misinformed." Now we were arriving in town.

Geri asked, "Is there anywhere I can catch a bus back home?"

I dropped her off at the G & G where the Valley Transit bus stops to board passengers. I wished her luck and wondered if this was how all this Visitant business had come about? I never did see the infamous black sequined gown and red shoes.

Could there be some truth to Twitty's assessment of the situation? A ghost sent to punish people for their misdeeds? Many people believe that mining uranium pollutes the environment and that we would have to face the consequences for disturbing Mother Nature. A Visitant? *¡Quien Sabe!* Who knows! For my part I simply avoid that stretch of road. Why take any chances…

A Well-Haunted Floodway

by Janice Workman

Santa Rosa, Texas

"I never look in my rearview mirror when I cross that bridge," Mary shared with me. I asked if she had heard of strange events occurring on the U.S. Highway 77 Floodway Bridge between Combes and Sebastian.

"I don't want to see her sitting in the backseat." she continued.

"Who?" I asked.

"There's this little girl who is supposed to appear in the backseat of the car just as you start across the bridge. If you look in the rearview mirror, they say you can see her. She never says anything, just sits and stares out the window. As soon as you get to the other side, she disappears."

"Have you ever seen her?" I asked.

"No, but my uncle knew a guy who saw her, and he said the car got really cold. Even fogged up the windows," Mary added with a shiver.

The stretch of road between the cities of Combes and Sebastian is typical of what folks think of when they think of South Texas. Cactus, sage brush, dirt roads winding away through ranch land, longhorn cattle grazing, watering holes in various stages of evaporation, all seen through the shimmer of heat waves coming off the blacktop. U.S. Highway 77 seems nothing more than a way of heading north, until you reach the

194

Floodway Bridge. Long-haul truckers and local commuters alike speak of the ghosts that frequent that quarter mile stretch.

The tale I heard most frequently was similar to the one Mary told me. A young girl materializes in the rear seat of the automobile when starting across the bridge from south to north. She looks about twelve years old with large dark eyes, long dark hair, and an old fashioned white dress with lace on the collar. She never says a word, doesn't smile or meet your eyes; she simply looks out the side window until the bridge is crossed on the north side. No one knows who she could be or where she is going, although it was suggested that she is one of Llorona's children looking for her mother.

La Llorona is a well-known figure in Mexican folklore. As with such tales, there are variations on the theme, but for the most part the story entails of a young widow with two children, living in a small village in the mountains of Mexico. At a town fiesta she met Juan, and fell in love. Juan said that he could never marry her. Believing this was because of the burden of raising children not his own, she led her children to the shore of a nearby lake and drowned them. On returning to Juan, she told him their problems were over and they could now be wed. Juan, on hearing what she had done, rejected her with a terrible rage. He loved the children, but his mother was ailing and needed him at home. That was the reason he could not marry her. Marie, overwhelmed by her loss of love and the realization of what she had done, returned to the lake. There she cried, calling for her dead children as she walked into the water and drowned. To this day, when you pass a body of water on a dark night you can hear La Llorona, 'the crying one', calling for her lost babies. Children are advised to mind their elders or Llorona will come for them instead.

Truck drivers have an altogether different account of spectral events on that same bridge. My husband worked as a diesel mechanic for years and was privy to gossip that truckers tend to keep amongst themselves.

"There used to be a bar named *'Aqui Mi Quedo'* (Here I'll Stay) at the other side of the bridge in Sebastian. It was a good place to stop before heading north, since there wasn't much else for miles. One evening a driver went in there to get a cola for himself and a GI that he had picked up hitchhiking south of the bridge. When he got to the register, he saw a picture of that same soldier on the wall behind the counter with a sign that said 'Pray for our troops'. He told the cashier he had their hometown hero in the cab of his truck and she started crying. Apparently Army officials and a telegram had arrived the day before with a posthumous Purple Heart for the soldier killed in combat. He dropped the cokes and ran back to the truck. There wasn't any sign of the GI or his army duffle. I think it was a while before he stopped to pick up anyone else!" Abe told me, and then added, "The bar's gone now, but there are people around here that remember it. I still hear about that guy in uniform sighted there every once in a while."

A report of a third apparition was relayed to me as well. I have no idea as to the validity of this story, where as the first two were told with a degree of sincerity and personal knowledge. I think it is only fair to the spirit to include her here, however, in the event there is truth in the telling.

In the late evening hours, a woman can be seen walking along Highway 77, headed south toward the bridge from Sebastian. She looks to be in her mid-twenties, wears a long skirt, has a shawl over dark black hair and carries a small cloth bag looped through her arm. If someone offers her a ride, she gets in and smiles, telling the driver, *"Gracias, voy a regresar a mi casa en El Rincon Del Diablo"* ("Thank you, I am going back to my house in The Den of the Devil"). As the car crosses the bridge, she repeatedly asks the driver if he has seen her children. Further down the road, she cries and wails, begging for "Los ninos." Now, I know that this story sounds a lot like Llorona, but as the driver nears the 107 exit to Santa Rosa the story takes a twist. From a lovely twenty-something senorita,

196

she starts to change. Her skin dries and cracks, clinging to her bones until she resembles a skeleton with her clothes hanging in decaying shreds. Her eyes begin to blaze red from a skull-like face framed in grey matted hair and her cries turn to howls and screeches. Death's Head Hawk moths fly from her crumbling handbag. With a final "Mi ninos, Mi ninos," she vanishes in a flash of sparks and sulfur.

Urban legend? Mexican Folk Lore? The result of too many Margaritas?

I don't know, you be the judge, but before there was Santa Rosa, there was the small town of "El Rincon Del Diablo" – The Den of the Devil.

Brownsville Haunted History Tour

by Ann Greenfield

Brownsville, Texas

On one of our girl trips, Sandra, Jan and I thought it would be fun to learn about the legends of a nearby city. It was Monday morning and we were traveling south toward Brownsville on Country Road 1847, better known to the locals as Parades Line.

We were in our usual talkative gab-mode, when I heard a lone siren and saw flashing red lights in my rear view mirror. "Oh great!" He came out of nowhere. Caught speeding by the Brownsville sheriff was not my idea of fun. Could it get any worse?

The black-and-white sheriff's car looked strange as it pulled up behind me. You know how sometimes the sun peeks through the clouds to illuminate just one spot? That's how the cruiser looked. The sunlight reflected off the windshield, fenders, and hood creating an eerie rainbow of color. My eyes watered at the intensity even though I wore sunglasses. I blinked away the tears and decided to search for the necessary documents; drivers' license and proof of insurance.

"Jan, will you hand me my purse... Thanks."

"Sandra, my insurance card." I pointed to the glove compartment. "It's in a red thing." She began to rummage through the papers.

"Is he coming?" I asked.

Jan peered out of the rear window. "I don't think so. It's hard to tell with the glare." She shaded her eyes. "No, no he's just sitting there."

Sandra handed me the red plastic cardholder and looked back. "Now he's standing by the door, but not moving."

I glanced in the side mirror, just a silhouette. It was creepy. The silhouette ambled toward my pearl Pathfinder, the morning sunlight radiated from behind him, and all I could make out was his western hat and a glint of the Texas star over his heart.

Tap Tap Tap...

When I lowered my window, a burst of cold air shot into my face. I gasped. Had the weather changed? A cold front? Usually October is still hot and humid in the Rio Grande Valley.

"Is there an emergency?"

"Uh..." I couldn't think of one. "No, Sir."

"Where are you girls headed today?" asked the sheriff.

"We're going to the Heritage Complex, to the ghost tour." I could see his nametag, but couldn't read the name. He didn't introduce himself. Usually officers identify themselves. At least they did on TV and in the movies.

"Do you ladies believe in... ghosts?" The sheriff slid his sunglasses toward the end of his nose and peered over the top of his sunglasses.

We paused and simultaneously shook our heads no.

"The reason I stopped you, ma'am," he drawled, "is that you ran the red light and you were traveling over the posted speed limit."

I swallowed hard. I knew it. The long stretch of road was isolated with no sign of life and the light was yellow when I approached the intersection. I gunned the engine to make it through before it turned red. Obviously, I didn't make it. Since there was really nothing I could say, I gave him my best repentant smile. "Oh, sorry officer."

"Drivers' license and insurance," he requested, matter-of-factly.

I handed him the requested documents.

"Mrs. Greenfield…"

I was prepared for a ticket. I couldn't take the driver's safety course again. It was too soon. Shoot! I'd have to pay the ticket.

"I'm going to let you off with a warning… this time," he said, to my surprise, and handed back my documents. "Slow down and drive safely."

"Thank you." I was relieved.

The sheriff tipped his hat. "Ma'am." He then turned and sauntered back to his sheriff's car.

I breathed a heavy sigh, "Thank goodness we didn't get a ticket."

"That was lucky." said Jan.

Like three carefree teenagers, we gave each other high-fives and burst into laughter.

I looked in the rear view mirror, "Man, he took off fast! It's only been a few seconds, where did he go?" I motioned to the girls. We all looked around.

"He just vanished," said Jan.

"There was something strange about that sheriff?" commented Sandra.

Yes, we all nodded in silence.

I realized we were alone on the now deserted road. No cop car. No other cars.

Only us. "Let's get out of here!" With a shiver, I pulled the car back on to Paredes Line Road to continue our journey.

We were specifically going to the 'Third Annual Haunted History Trolley Tour' hosted by the city of Brownsville. It's the southern-most city in Texas and sits in the 'V' created by the Gulf of Mexico and Mexico.

The tour promised tales of ghost sightings throughout the city, along with stops at some of the city's most haunted spots: the Cameron County Court House, Fort Brown and of course, the old Brownsville City Cemetery.

We decided on the seven o'clock tour, since even with Day Light Savings, it would be dark. We wanted it to be a little spooky, besides ghosts don't come out in the daylight, do they?

We spent the rest of the day exploring Brownsville, shopping across the Mexican border in Matamoros, and finished with an early supper.

By the time we arrived at the Heritage Center, it was dark and the moon peeked over the downtown buildings casting gloomy shadows on the darkened tour bus.

"Hey look, no trolleys. Shoot!" I couldn't help my disappointment. Since the previous tours used trolleys, I was looking forward to riding in one. No luck! This year it was a city bus, not quite the same charm.

"At least they're air conditioned," said Jan. The temperature in the Rio Grande Valley was ninety or above, ten plus months out of the year.

I was antsy waiting in line to buy tickets. I decided to break the boredom, "How many ghosts can y'all name?" I asked. Both Sandra and Jan rolled their eyes at me.

"Casper the friendly ghost," Jan smirked.

"There's the ghosts of Christmas past, present, and future," said Sandra. "But I couldn't say if Charles Dickens actually saw the ghosts or if they were a figment of his imagination."

"Okay, a cartoon and a fictional character. Ooooo. Are y'all afraid yet?" I held up my hands and wiggled my fingers to indicate ghosts. We giggled.

We bought our tickets, boarded the tour bus, and found seats near the back.

"Soooo do you think we'll see an apparition?" I drew the word out in my best rendition of a television ghost. They pretended to shiver.

Our laughter was interrupted when a man dressed in a soldier's costume tapped XXthe microphone, "Good evening." The heritage officer began the tour, "A warning... tonight you may see some strange things. How many of you believe in ghosts?"

Jan leaned in and whispered, "Most people don't believe in ghosts. I know I don't."

"Me either," said Sandra.

The tour stopped at the first scheduled place, but no ghosts appeared at the courthouse. Not even the shimmer of the harvest moon through the clouds brought out were-wolves.

The next place was Fort Brown. "Many people have reported hearing cannon fire and observed soldiers fighting," said our host. Again, no soldiers manifested themselves and no other specters or ghosts appeared.

Our host continued to entertain us with stories and history. Amusing, but still no one in the tour encountered a sighting. Nothing extraordinary happened. We weren't surprised and didn't expect to see or experience any kind of apparitions, friendly or otherwise, so why were we disappointed? Because we really wanted to believe that something else could be out there, an after-life perhaps?

The last stop was the old Brownsville City Cemetery. We were still optimistic in our quest for ghost sightings. "If ghosts lived anywhere, it would be here!" whispered Sandra.

"Anything slimy touch your cheek?" I touched my hand to my cheek as we disembarked. "Cold wind... chill the back of your neck?" I raised my eyebrows and shrugged. We stifled a giggle.

Gravel crunched under our shoes as we gathered by the six-foot high brick fence. Away from the down town lights, the cemetery was panther black. The wrought iron gates were unlocked and the mesquite trees filtered moon light into dancing figures on the elaborate monuments and historic tombstones. You could smell the pungent water from the town Resaca.

Our tour guide leaned against the wall and broke the silence with several stories. One in particular hit close to home.

"Some years ago a sheriff was killed by a drunk driver on Paredes Line Road. Whether day or night, if you speed or run the red light, a ghost sheriff will stop you. You may even see his black and white patrol car. If the ghost sheriff stops you... he only gives you a warning. Then he disappears into thin air. No police car. No taillights. No sheriff. Nothing. Not even mist or fog, like you see in the movies to indicate it was a ghost."

Everyone else laughed at the movie comment, but Sandra, Jan and I looked at each other. Our hearts pounded in our chest and our faces drained of color. "Wasn't it Paredes Line Road where the sheriff stopped us?" I whispered, my throat was dry and I could barely form the words. Sandra and Jan nodded yes. Their eyes were wide and glassy.

"Should we say something?" asked Jan.

The hairs on the back of my neck tingled and I shivered. "Let's get out of here!" We scampered back to the safety of the bus and didn't say a word the remainder of the tour.

I didn't speed until I hit Interstate 83, the fastest way home, and was well out of Brownsville. None of us spoke until Harlingen. Then we all said the same thing, "There really are ghosts!" Would anyone believe us?

I know it sounds crazy. Ghosts don't exist. Right? That's what I would have said yesterday, but today I know differently. My mind was changed that October night. I believe ghosts *do* come out in the daylight!

In Brownsville, Texas, a ghost sheriff patrols Paredes Line Road for the safety of motorists like you and me. He appears out of nowhere and disappears into thin air. If you commit an infraction of the law... you, too, may see him.

The Ghost Cow of
Farm Road 511

by Jan Holmes Frost

Brownsville, Texas

This legendary story is most often told from the viewpoint of one of the people involved... Fernando Vargas. Here is how the story has been passed down, in his words, for ages in south Texas...

I am Fernando Diego Vargas and I tell you this story because many times late at night, when it is safe, *la vaca pinta*, the spotted cow, crosses Farm Road 511 in Brownsville, Texas. If you see her, do not fear, for she is a harmless *fantasma*. I believe it to be her sainted mission to keep vehicles from injuring innocent children like my friends and me. They are, Isabel Castillo and Paolo Sanchez. This is our story...

One day I am walking my cow home from the field. She is taller than me because I am only a boy. Sometime I ride on la Pinta's back. I know she likes this because she always walks faster. But not tonight, as we must cross the dangerous Farm Road 511. It is late and my father will scold me if I miss dinner. My mama, she cooks and cleans all day. It is disrespectful to be the last one seated at the table. I hurry with the cow, but tonight she is slow. "Come Pinta, I will be in trouble because of you."

There is a way to get home more quickly, but it is not so wise. This time I will be very careful as I cross Farm Road 511. Then the spotted cow stops. She has stopped in the middle of the road. I pull on her rope, but she does not come. "Hurry, Pinta, you will get us run over."

A truck comes speeding towards us and I think it will hit la Pinta, so I wave my arms and yell. The truck tries to miss us, but then I am flying through the air. I don't see any more after that. Now out of the blackness I return to observe but I'm unable to touch or feel because now I am a *fantasma*.

The next day I see my mother is screaming, "Kill the *vaca loca*. She is the devil, the *vaca diabolica*. Look what she has done to *mijito*, Fernando."

"No, *mí amor*," my father says, "she is a good cow...for someone else to have."

"Tell them," mama screams, "tell them it is a devil cow."

"Sí, I will. You must rest. Take an *aqua salada*, it will calm you."

My father and my little brother Juan, takes *la Pinta* to our friend and neighbor Señor Castillo. He lives two miles down the road from us. It is a long walk and Juan cries, so father lets him ride on Pinta's back. I think she likes this because she walks faster.

We are greeted by Señor Castillo and my father says, "Mí amigo, I have brought you a gift. We have many cows, but my wife does not want this one. She says it is why our son was hit by a truck and is dead. A silly woman's idea, but I cannot kill a good milk cow."

"Sí, I understand. My wife also believes cows are demons. Thank you, I will take good care of this cow, mí amigo."

The Castillos have three daughters who are my friends, Isabel, Leticia, and Celeste. The next day Señor Castillo tells Celeste, "Mijita, you will help Lety with the cow. Take it to the field, but do not cross the road until you come to the arroyo. Be careful and come back quickly to finish your chores."

Senior Castillo is a wise father, but I myself will watch out for *mi amigas*.

Every morning before school, Isabel and Lety lead the cow to the field. At the arroyo they meet the school bus. After school they cross the road to bring la Pinta home to the barn.

A year has passed and now Isabel goes with her older sisters to school. Isabel is very small and walks slowly, so Celeste and Lety lift her up to ride on the wide back of la Pinta. The cow likes this and walks faster.

One day it is raining when the school bus stops at the arroyo and I see that a flash flood is coming. I watch as my three *amigas* get off the bus into water over their knees. Then the bus goes forward and it is caught up in a frightening wave of water that comes racing down the arroyo. The girls watch in horror as their school bus is lifted up and carried away in the torrent.

"Run. Run quickly," I cry out. But of course they cannot hear me.

Above the noise of the water, Lety yells, "Come, *mís hermanítas*, we must run before the water sweeps us away." They hold hands and wade down the road together as I try to hurry them along. But it does me no good. I am helpless.

"Wait. We must bring la Pinta home," Isabel cries. "Father would not want us to leave her. She may also be taken away by this storm."

"No, it is not safe," Lety shouts to Isabel. "Leave the *vaca* and come home with us."

But Isabel does not listen. She lets go of her sister's hand and crosses the road to the field. Afraid for their lives, Celeste and Lety race home to tell their father.

"I must go," Señor Castillo says, and he pulls on his boots and runs out of the house.

Isabel ties a long rope on Pinta and shoos her out of the gate. "We will go down to the crossroad and it will be better. No so much water."

Isabel cannot see through the wall of rain. Thinking it is safe to cross, she and la Pinta walk to the middle of the road. Then she hears a loud horn. "Come, mí Pinta, we must run or we'll get hit by a truck," she cries.

Then the crazy cow stops, just like she did with me, Fernando Diego Vargas. Isabel begins to scream. She too is flying through the air and I catch her because she too has become a spirit.

"My baby, my Isabel. God and the saints above, look what has happened because of that demon cow. I will shoot it myself," Señora Castillo screams, as she grabs her husband's gun that hangs high on their wall.

"No, no, I will do it," Señor Castillo insists and he takes the gun from his weeping wife's hands.

But Celeste and Lety do not want their father to kill la Pinta and they plead with him, "No, Papa, let us give the cow to Grandfather. He will take care of it. He needs a cow. He said so the other day. Please?" Lety weeps. And Celeste cries to her father, "It is not the cow's doing that Isabel had died. Do not kill la Pinta. It is not what Isabel would want."

The next day the rain stops and they find the school bus is found. It has floated all the way to the Gulf of Mexico, which isn't very far. The children on the bus are rescued and no one is hurt.

Señor Castillo leads Pinta along the side of Farm Road 511 to his father's land which is two miles away. Lety and Celeste stay at home to comfort their mother so Isabel and I seat our ghostly selves atop Pinta's back. I know she likes this as she walks faster.

We arrive at Grandfather Castillo's and Senior Castillo says, "Here is a gift for you, Papa. She is a good cow, not the *vaca loca* that my wife insists. You take her. You need a cow."

Señor Castillo lives alone since his wife died. Paolo Sanchez, a neighbor boy, comes every day to help the old man. Paolo's mother has also died and he lives with his father and his sister, Josefina. Paolo misses his mother very much. She was beautiful and gentle.

Paolo goes to work at Señor Castillo's barn and is greeted by the spotted cow. He likes her immediately.

"This is my new cow, Paolo. She is given to me by my son, Ernesto."

"Sí, Señor. I am aware of the accident on road 511."

"Sí, sí, they call her *la vaca loca*. I don't think this cow has a demon. Look in her eyes, there is no devil there."

Paolo pulls the cow's head down and looks in both of its large brown eyes. He agrees with Señor Castillo.

"Do you want me to take this cow to feed on your land?" Paolo asks.

"Sí, you do that, but beware of the crazy drivers on the road," Señor Castillo warns. "Oh, and they call the vaca, Pinta."

"Gracias, I will take good care of la Pinta."

A year has passed and people seldom think of the vaca loca except sometimes they will see Paolo leading la Pinta to Señor Castillo's barn and they are reminded of what happened to me, Fernando Diego Vargas and to little Isabel Castillo.

I hear as Paolo talks to the cow when they travel to and from the field.

Paolo says, "At least you listen to me, mí Pinta, not like my father and sister who ignore me. My mother was a good woman, and I don't know why the Lord took her. Her name was Marisol. She had long black hair that would swish across my face when she hugged me. Her eyes were very warm, like yours, mí Pinta. I think she watches me through your eyes. What do you see, mí Pinta?"

La Pinta must like this because she walks faster.

One day Paolo tells Pinta more about Marisol. "In the summer she would serve us giant strawberries covered with fresh cream. It is good of Señor Castillo to share your milk with us so we may still have *la crema*."

Now Paolo is fifteen and his father allows him to drive the tractor. Pinta watches from her field across Farm Road 511. It is late in the afternoon and time for Paolo to bring her to the barn. The sun is setting and oranges and yellows shine across the pond next to the field.

"Mí Pinta, how was your day? Are you ready to return to your safe barn?" Paolo asks.

The cow nods. Paolo pats her nose and feeds her a carrot. He loves the cow's scent as he strokes her neck.

Darkness is closing in on Paolo and the cow. "Dusk is not a good time to be crossing the road, Pinta. In the daylight it is clear to see if any trucks are coming, unless it is raining," he says. "I tell you the truth; late at night is the very best time to cross, when you can see the lights of oncoming vehicles. But this time, dusk, is not so good, especially with the setting sun in our eyes."

I watch in anticipation as Paolo leads the cow to their usual crossing and looks in both directions. It is safe, or so he thinks. I want to tell him to wait. Halfway across the road they hear the blaring of a horn and the squeal of brakes as a large pickup truck comes shooting out of a nearby driveway.

It is too late to run. Paolo holds up his hand as though to ward off the careening vehicle. In slow motion he watches the dirty red truck veer to the right. Then the driver loses control, and through the dust Paolo sees the magnified headlights, bug splattered grill, and the roaring engine is coming directly at him.

He opens his mouth to cry out a warning to la Pinta. Then he feels something hit him. He is knocked off his feet and lands face down in thorny weeds along the side of the road. There is a sharp pain in his head and he doesn't see any more after that.

Paolo wakes up in a strange room. He hears a beeping sound and his head hurts. He is in the hospital. Then he remembers the truck coming at him on Farm Road 511.

The next day Paolo is better and he goes home. When he asks his father about the truck and about la Pinta, his father shakes his head and says, "Mijito, that is not a vaca loca, like people have always said."

"Sí, Papa, I know that. Is la Pinta hurt?"

"The cow is gone. She was hit by the truck, but she is a vaca santa. The driver tells us that he cannot keep his truck in control and your cow, the sainted vaca, stepped forward and pushed you out of the way. She saved your life, my son."

Paolo can see tears in his father's eyes. "She is out in the field, past the burial place. We put her not far from your mother."

Paolo walks to his mother's grave from where he can see the mound of fresh earth that covers la Pinta.

"Mother, how will I know if it is your spirit that saved me from being killed?"

He doesn't expect an answer, but he feels a calming sensation and sees his mother's warm eyes and la Pinta's knowing gaze.

I am Fernando Diego Vargas and I tell you this story because many times late at night, when it is safe, my cow, la Pinta, crosses Farm Road 511 in Brownsville. I believe it is her sainted mission to stop vehicles from hurting innocent children like us, but she won't hurt you…she's a harmless ghost cow.

The Legend of La Llorona
by Sandra Vela

Brownsville, Texas

Several sightings of *La Llorona* (lah yoh-roh-nah) or weeping woman have occurred around Brownsville, Texas, near where the Rio Grande River bordering Mexico runs just a few yards from the Old Texas Military Highway. Those who have actually seen her describe her as a beautiful woman wearing flowing white garments that shimmer in the night. Her head is covered and she wears a gleaming *rebozo* (shawl) around her shoulders. She looks helpless, lost, wandering alone in a confused state. She calls out for someone to help her find her children. Alarmed by the thought that children may be drowning in the nearby river, people have attempted to help the weeping woman, only to see her enter the water and disappear.

When she reveals her face, some have reported that her eyes ooze bloody tears. She covers her face and claws at her eyes in anguish. This is the most frightening detail reported of the apparition.

People who live in the Brownsville area have heard her cries on foggy nights, but few have dared to venture out to investigate because they know the legend of the weeping woman. Almost everyone you speak with has heard of her or has a relative or friend who had an encounter with *La Llorona*.

The most common manifestation of *La Llorona* is the sound of a woman weeping at night. Sometimes it is a soft, inconsolable sobbing, which is more pitiful than frightening. This is a cry of despair. It weighs heavily on the hearts of those who can hear her, but cannot help her. They believe her cry is a warning to stay away. Her grief is all encompassing, able to swallow a living person in its depths like the muddy waters of the Rio Grande River. More often, people report hearing loud spine chilling wails and howls of a woman in distress echoing through the mist at the water's edge. People have approached the sight certain that someone is drowning or being attacked only to find nothing.

No one knows, for sure, who the weeping woman is, but there are many possible explanations offered by those who believe in her. The reasons why she drowned her children account for the most variety in this story. The most common account of her haunting is that she is a malevolent spirit, beaconing disobedient children to the water's edge only to grab them and plunge them into the water to their deaths just as she had done with her own children. She serves as a warning to mothers to take care of their children and to children to obey their parents.

Some see her as a pitiful, lonely spirit, forever doomed in search of the innocent victims, who drowned at her hands, because she could not see any other way out of her circumstances. In this version, she wants other mothers to grieve as she has grieved through the ages, to feel the anguish of her loss, so they too will know how it feels to lose their children and realize that she has paid the ultimate price for her sin.

Legend claims that she appears as a warning to women who forget their place in the patriarchal Hispanic society where a man's job is to keep his woman in check or risk an unforgivable assault on his machismo. Her only job is to care for his house and his needs and to give him children. *La Llorona* may well have been a woman who didn't heed this lesson and thus paid the ultimate price for her weakness, for her pride, for her jealousy, for her passion, or for her desires. In this version, she drowns her children out of rage against her husband who represents the yoke that has kept her dependent and victimized to the point that she could no longer cope. In the end, she regrets the unforgivable thing that she has done, and so she punishes herself with eternal grief. The stories try to explain why she appears near water or along lonely roads.

Recently, several modern day *Lloronas* have been documented, not as spirits, but as real women, eerily with the same story. We've all heard the true story of Susan Smith who allegedly strapped her two small children into their car seats of her Mazda and let it roll quietly into John D. Long Lake in South Carolina. She later appeared on TV crying and sobbing for the return of her babies. Only later did she confess that she did it because she wanted to have a relationship with a man who didn't want the children. Then there was Andrea Yates, a mother of six who allegedly systematically drowned her children in the bathtub and laid them neatly on the bed covered by a sheet until her husband came home. She was later found not guilty, by reason of insanity, due to the fact that she was suffering from depression. What unimaginable desperation might have possessed these women to allegedly commit the ultimate act of filicide? Ponder that, and you may begin to understand the story of *La Llorona*.

One can say she weeps for all these tragic victims a warning to us all. She bares the unrelenting guilt and pain of a woman who made the wrong choices in life, forever cursed to cry in the night along riverbanks and *resacas* (river inlets), mourning the innocent victims.

Many who have heard the story may not believe that it is true, but those who have had encounters with this spirit know that she does exist and continues to haunt the waterways of the Rio Grande Valley.

213

"He Left the Road at Ninety"

by Mona D. Sizer

Reynosa, Texas

This story was told to the author by Allen Damron...

We were just a bunch of teenagers back in 1956. Mitch was barely fifteen. His driver's license was a "learner." And his mother didn't even know he had it. Like most farm kids he'd been taking his daddy's pickup out since he was twelve. Now the pickup had a set of stripped gears. It only did fifty-eight with the pedal to the floor, but he preferred to drive it instead of his mother's Buick. He told his friends it wouldn't corner in any space smaller than a church parking lot. And he complained mightily that it was just like driving a hearse.

Mitch longed for a T-Bird. Now there was a beautiful car. He would have drooled all over the steering wheel of a new Corvette, but even to imagine one was beyond his wildest dreams. For now he kept his father's pickup gassed and drove like a crazy man whenever he got out of sight of the house. Truth to tell, he always wanted to go faster than the car in front of him. His compulsion made for some hair-raising moments on the two-lane farm-to-market roads in the Rio Grande Valley in the mid 1950s.

Coming back from Mexico, drunk from too many Carta Blancas, we should have known better than to let Mitch drive. But nobody would ever have thought to take the keys away because it was dangerous for him to drive drunk. Even as he

214

threw the old pickup into gear, stomped the gas, and roared out of Reynosa, the three of us just yelled like banshees. I pounded the door on my side, and Mitch drove with one hand on the wheel and pounded on his.

We cleared the bridge and tore past the pump house in Hidalgo. Mitch slid sideways through the stop sign onto U.S. Highway 281 from San Antonio to Brownsville, the old Military Highway, and we were heading east, the moon lighting up the road like day and the fields flashing by us.

I didn't care where I was. I just leaned back and listened to the engine roaring and the wind tearing my hair and thought nothing at all. Halfway to Brownsville the Y with the canal on one side came up all of a sudden.

"Look out!" I yelled.

Joe Bob, sitting in the middle, raised his head, and he yelled too.

We both had an instant to look at Mitch as he twisted the wheel too hard to the right.

The pickup fishtailed.

As we plowed up the embankment, he must have over-corrected. At the top of the levee, we went airborne.

I'd have lost my arm if we hadn't flipped back left. Then we were rolling over. I don't quite know how it all happened, except I ended up on top of the heap. Joe Bob's shoulder clipped my chin. I was seeing stars, and he was under me pushing and kicking. I tried to draw a breath and choked and strangled. My face was in the water. That's when I realized the pickup was upside down in the damn canal!

I reached for the door, pulled myself through the window, and dragged Joe Bob with me. He fell out into the water. I hoped he'd make it to the bank. Then I went back in for Mitch. He was grunting and still thrashing around, but I got his shirt collar and dragged his head above the water. He started yelling the minute he could blow the water out of his mouth and nose. Yelling and moaning and coughing. And bleeding. By the

215

moonlight I could see his head was cut open. I was so scared I wet my pants.

Thank God! I was already wet.

I heard Joe Bob splashing around. "Can't get a grip," he cried. "Bank's too slippery. Can't get a damn grip."

I looked around and all I could see was the canal banks on both sides of us, steep and slippery. No way were we going to able to climb out.

And what was worse: no way were we going to be able to explain this to Mitch's dad.

Joe Bob managed to climb back on the pickup and was standing up screaming and waving his arms. I saw the lights of a car coming, but it couldn't see us. No. The bank was too high. Nobody could see us waving unless we actually climbed out and stood up in plain sight. We were going to have to make it out by ourselves.

Joe Bob tried jumping, but only once. The pickup shuddered underneath us and slid forward. Joe Bob lost his balance and fell back on top of me. I almost lost my grip on Mitch.

Oh, God! We couldn't do that again.

"We gotta come up with something else," I grunted. "We've got to get out of here before the whole thing sinks."

But we couldn't get out. The pickup settled still farther at a crazy angle. Fortunately, it didn't sink any more. All Joe Bob and I could do was balance on it with our feet in the water and hold Mitch's head, so he could breathe. Occasionally, a car would drive by, and we'd yell at the top of our lungs, but they never slowed.

As it was beginning to get daylight, an old truck came creeping along. He was going so slow that he heard he and us stopped. We kept yelling and calling and begging and cheering. The old Mexican farmer climbed up on top of the bank. He stared down but didn't seem to recognize the situation at first. It was still dark inside the canal, but we waved, and he waved back. Fortunately, he had a rope, so we could climb out. It took the three of us to drag our buddy out. The bleeding had stopped by that time, but all three of us were covered in Mitch's blood.

I wrote my phone number on a piece of paper and gave the old man some money. He drove off back down the road to a place where he knew there was a telephone. While we waited, I threw up and then I stood and shivered until my dad finally got there. He'd passed the ambulance. I was never so glad to see anyone in my life.

Mitch didn't drive for a year. His dad kept his keys in his pocket, and his mother kept hers in her purse. Finally, he turned sixteen when he could get his license legally to drive farm vehicles and such. During that whole year he talked about the wreck a lot to anyone who would listen. He swore he'd been doing ninety when a tire had blown. He was sure a tire had blown. That was what made him lose it.

We didn't say anything. We didn't contradict him. If he wanted to believe that, it was his business and not anybody else's.

But, finally, his dad bought him a used pickup with the understanding that he was supposed to help with the cotton and grain harvests and drive to and from school. He absolutely couldn't take it and go get drunk in Mexico. On the very same day my folks gave me a long talking-to, and the upshot was that I wasn't supposed to get in the pickup with Mitch ever again.

Joe Bob told me his folks had told him the same thing.

Of course, when your folks tell you you're not supposed to do something, what are you going to do? Soon as we could, we sneaked off and went riding with Mitch in his new-used pickup.

That road and that canal had been preying on Mitch's mind, so nothing would do but we would go look at the canal. Once we pulled off to the side of the road, he got out and climbed the bank. We didn't bother to follow him up. We didn't want to see it. My mother had impressed me with tears in her eyes how I'd almost drowned. Other than the water and the weeds, there was really nothing much to see. Even the ruts where the pickup had ripped up the embankment were gone, washed away by the hurricane rains we'd had that summer.

As we stood there, he kept saying over and over that he was sure it was the blown tire. He was sure.

The next year I was a senior and had football practice after school. Coach was strict about his players not breaking training and drinking. I was counting on playing football in college, so it pretty much finished me with Mitch, who was still heading for Mexico every chance he got. When I couldn't go with him, and Joe Bob didn't much want to go, he took up with some younger guys who'd spread the stories about how crazy he was.

They thought it was fun, they said. But they didn't quite meet my eyes when they said it. Once in a while, someone would break down and admit that Mitch kept running off the road at the Y.

"Just won't slow down," I overheard one of them say. He giggled sort of nervous-like. "Just keeps saying that he can make it. Says his tire blew. Caused the only wreck he ever had."

All I could think about was sitting up on the underside of his daddy's pickup staring at four good, fully inflated tires. I didn't say anything. You don't rat on your buddy even if he is "full of it."

But in the end I kinda wished I'd said something. Might not have done any good, but then again it might have.

Everyone heard the story just three weeks shy of the end of the school year.

Mitch and a couple of his *compadres* had been coming back from Reynosa. They said he hadn't been drinking, but we all knew that just wasn't so.

Mitch. Go to Mexico and not drink? Tell me another one!

218

Somehow he'd lost control and slid into the Y again. This time the car had fishtailed the other way and lost it completely. Mitch was thrown half out of the car. On the first roll, he was underneath it, half in, half out. His left arm, shoulder, and head left a bloody mess on the highway.

The other two kids walked away with a broken arm, some knocked out teeth, and mild concussions between them.

Before the funeral I said to Joe Bob, "Do you reckon another tire blew out?"

He just shook his head. I put my arm around his shoulder and we shivered and shook and held on tight for a minute.

When we graduated, we knew we were going separate ways. The chances were good that we'd just meet on occasion when we happened to be back in the Valley at the same time on vacations and such.

For old time's sake, we decided to take a couple of dates and go over to Reynosa. We were all eighteen. I was just a couple of weeks short of my nineteenth birthday. There wasn't any place to celebrate being adults in Mercedes, Texas.

I borrowed my mother's car, a new Pontiac with air conditioning. The girls got all dressed up, and we drove over the bridge like a bunch of old people going out for dinner and dancing.

After midnight we drove across the bridge out of Reynosa. In the rearview mirror I could see Joe Bob getting it on with his girl, pretty hot and heavy. I was glad he was having good time, but I was sort of disappointed. We'd had fun, but we hadn't had that much fun. My date had her head snuggled down on my shoulder. I was pretty sure she'd dozed off. Never should have brought her that second frozen daiquiri.

I'd behaved myself because I was driving. Being responsible was not that much fun either. The radio was playing something by Pat Boone. My mind started drifting back. I checked my rearview mirror again.

219

Suddenly, a pair of headlights flashed on behind me. Coming fast. The road was pretty narrow and up ahead was the Y.

I felt a chill run through me. I straightened up keeping my eyes on those headlights. The driver came on – pedal to the metal. He was going to rear-end me. As quick as I dared, I drove the car onto the shoulder.

He missed me by a whisker when he pulled alongside.

I scowled at the face illuminated by the dashboard light.

Mitch?

It couldn't be. It wasn't. It wasn't. Whoever-it-was stomped the accelerator and the pickup flashed by me, swerving as it headed for the Y.

I braked and heard someone else's brakes squeal. Before my eyes I watched the pickup rocket up the side of the canal, roll at the top, and disappear over the embankment.

My eyes met Joe Bob's in the rearview mirror. He'd seen it too.

I let the car roll to a stop. Gently, I moved my date's head from my shoulder and opened the car door.

"Where're you going?"

I couldn't say where I was going or why or what I was going to do. I felt a strange cold chill and a compulsion I couldn't resist. "Back in a minute."

Joe Bob joined me at the top of the canal bank. Together we looked down into the dark water. Still as a mirror, reflecting the stars and the half moon. Undisturbed.

"Did you see it?" Joe Bob whispered.

"Yeah."

"What do you think it was?"

"I don't know what to think."

"I don't think we both saw the same thing that wasn't there." His voice broke. "What do you think?"

I couldn't think of anything to say for a minute. Then I shrugged. "I think Mitch still can't make that curve."

Every so often strange reports will come back from the Y on the old Military Highway at certain times of the night. Of course, very few cars follow that route any more – with expressways shooting across the Valley north and south, east and west. But perhaps some night after midnight, if someone ventures along that stretch of road, he might see more than he bargained for.

Doing Our Part

by Mona D. Sizer

Raymondville, Texas

On December 7, 1941, World War II started for me at a birthday party for one of my closest friends. I was only seven years old, and Thalia Gayle, the honoree, had just turned seven. What a fateful birthday that was about to become!

The party had barely started when my mother brought the news. She was the telephone operator working the switchboard. Though we hated for her to work on Sunday, we needed the extra time-and-a-half paid on what was supposed to be a day of rest. She was the first to know about the disaster, and she came straight from work to be sure I was safe and to tell L. C. and Helen Smith, Thalia Gayle's father and mother.

The party that had hardly begun finished rather quickly as more and more people arrived. No one knew what was going to happen next. Would the Japanese that had bombed Pearl Harbor on the island of Hawaii soon be sending planes to drop bombs on California, on Texas, on Washington, D.C.? No one knew, but everyone was concerned.

Even before the sun sank behind the horizon and the December temperature chilled, parents took their children home. It was just as well. The party had long been over for everyone.

We soon found out how everything was going to change for everyone. Just before Christmas, Uncle Jack came to see us.

The sight of him drove me into ecstasies of excitement. He was so beautiful in his forest green uniform with all the brass buttons. Even though he was a farmer with an essential job, he'd joined the army to "do his part." His brother Oslin had joined with him. His brother A. Y. had joined the Army Air Force. Three Damron sons – at twenty-two Jack was the youngest – were all going in harm's way, doing their part.

My grandmother picked up his son Allen, my little cousin just two years old, and held him so tightly he squeaked. I felt cold all over as a glimmer of what might happen to him dawned in my brain.

Everywhere I kept hearing the phrase "doing our part." I wanted to do my part too. Fortunately, Robert E. Lee Elementary School gave me an opportunity. Everybody bought Defense Stamps on Fridays. The ten and twenty-five cents we gave for the stamps went to buy guns and ammunition and all sorts of supplies for the armed forces.

Since my mother worked at the telephone office where the town's siren was located, I was really proud that she would probably be the one to blow it to warn of an air raid by incoming Japanese planes. I soon decided that she was an Air Raid Warden as well as a telephone operator. She was "doing her part."

The only one who couldn't think or find a single way to "do her part" was my grandmother. In fact, her life went on pretty much as usual. Her bi-monthly trips to Harlingen were deemed necessary because Raymondville had no library, and Allen and I had to have books.

Despite gasoline and rubber rationing, Mother and Mammaw agreed that no war should be allowed to interfere with our education. The library was in Harlingen, so we would drive the twenty-two miles, check out ten books, and come back. Two weeks later we would go back to turn them in and check out ten more.

Twice a month Mammaw would drive the narrow concrete strip that comprised old U.S. Highway 77 in her old dilapidated Chevrolet. The way was so familiar that we never noticed the fields of cotton and grain, the pastures with beef cattle, milk cows, and a few horses.

By 1942 what Mammaw came to notice, however, were the soldiers and sailors, airmen, and even a few marines hitchhiking to and from the bases in Harlingen and Corpus Christi. We didn't know they were most likely on their way to and from Mexico for a look at a different country and a "high-old time" before going into combat where chances were good some would be maimed or killed.

For a long time Mammaw drove right on by them. I thought she didn't stop and pick them up because she was ashamed of our dilapidated car. I didn't know she thought giving a ride might not be ladylike as well as possibly dangerous. She was a fifty-six-year-old woman with an eight-year-old girl and a four-year-old boy with no man to drive us. She didn't know what the service men would think – or do.

Until the day it rained. Not just a light, drifting, warm rain, but a cloudburst with thunder and lightning pelting a pair of boys in blue bell-bottom trousers, who stood like drowned puppies by the roadside.

Mammaw's tender heart couldn't leave them. She pulled over, put on the brake, and nodded for me to open the door.

Apologizing for being so wet, they pulled off their white caps and crawled into the backseat. I was delighted and Allen was ecstatic. He always rode there alone standing on the hump formed by the driveshaft. Now two grown men shared the space with him. Allen hadn't seen his father for such a long time. The very fact that he was close to two male adults in uniform was a thrill. For the first time, he actually sat down on the seat between them and tried to look older and taller.

One of the boys was so handsome, I was instantly reduced to speechlessness, introduced them both to Mammaw.

"I'm Able Seaman Arnold Patterson, Ma'am. This here's Able Seaman Ron Henderson. I'm from Oklahoma, and Ron here's from New Jersey." He grinned. "But we don't hold that against him."

Mammaw smiled warily. I smiled too. Seaman Patterson had red hair and freckles. Instantly, I became certain that I would someday marry a boy with red hair. Possibly Arnold, since he was from Oklahoma. He might know my Uncle Orr.

"Are you from Heavener?" I asked.

Mammaw shushed me, but he just shook his head. "Sorry to say I don't know where that is. I'm from Woodward."

"I'm only going to Harlingen," Mammaw told them defensively.

"That's okay," Arnold replied. "We appreciate getting out of the rain."

They told her they were going to Brownsville. I told them we were going to the library and why. They smiled and nodded.

They were impressive, spotlessly clean, and sporting fresh haircuts and shaves. They said, "Yes, Ma'am," to Mammaw. When she let them out under the canopy at the Sinclair station, they said, "Thank you, Ma'am, and much obliged."

Allen looked like he wanted to go with them. He climbed up in the seat and waved through the back window as we pulled away.

Wheels began to turn in my grandmother's mind. They had accepted the ride she offered and not said anything but thanks. They had been grateful not critical.

At last! At last! She had found a way to "do her part." She could give the boys rides.

Back home I greeted Mother at the door with the news. "We gave some sailors rides," I bubbled. "It was raining and we kept them from getting wet. They were from Oklahoma and New Jersey."

Mother looked at Mammaw as if she'd lost her mind. "Mother! You didn't pick up hitchhikers!"

"Oh, no," I said instantly. "They were sailors."

"*Mother!*"

Mammaw folded her arms. Her mouth set in a tight, straight line. "They needed rides. Everybody should do it. It's our duty."

Mother couldn't find fault with her patriotism, but she looked down at me. "Are you teaching her to do something dangerous?"

I couldn't figure out why it was dangerous. The boys were so nice. But I held my breath.

Mammaw shook her head. "It's for the War Effort," she said, as if that settled the argument. Then she added more softly, "It's the only thing I can do. I have to do my part too."

Mother didn't say another word.

For two years my grandmother picked up hitchhiking sailors, soldiers, airmen, and marines, carried them twenty miles on their journeys and let them out with "good luck and take care of yourselves."

A few times we picked up Ron and Arnold, whose red hair was a bright as ever. He even waved my grandmother down a couple of times when he recognized the old car. Sometimes we had as many as five riding with us. Four would crowd into the backseat and one would sit in the front holding Allen in his lap while I sat against Mammaw's side. While I held her purse, my long skinny legs had to straddle the gear shift on the floor of the Chevy.

Then we came to realize that we hadn't seen Arnold in quite a while. When we picked up Ron accompanied by another boy, we learned Arnold had shipped out.

That was the last time we saw Ron. "I guess he shipped out too," my grandmother said in a sad voice.

Then, one day during a pelting rain as the early winds of a hurricane swept its way in from the Gulf, Mammaw suddenly turned the wheel and began to pull over. "Look," she cried. "Look! I do believe I see Arnold. Oh, yes, it's Arnold."

"Where?" I reared up in the seat, but I couldn't see anyone. Just a mesquite tree and a cotton trailer with one wheel broken down by the side of road.

"Over there." She nodded smiling looking steadily off to the side of the road. She took her hand off the steering wheel to wave. The car lurched and she looked ahead to steady it. As the car rolled to a stop, she reached for the emergency brake.

"I don't see anybody," I said.

"Of course, you do. See." She pointed.

I looked intently, but I still didn't see anyone.

Mammaw sat there smiling, and then she stiffened and bit her lips. Her face went white and then she shifted noisily, released the brake, and drove on. When she got to the Sinclair station where she usually left her passengers out, she stopped and went in to inquire. The attendant came out to "fill 'er up" while she talked with the owner.

She came out dabbing at her face with her handkerchief. She had a grim, sad look on her face. When I asked what was wrong, she just shook her head. The three of us sat silent as we drove the rest of the way to the library.

Later I heard her tell Mother that so many, many boys were dying in this awful war. Many were dying overseas, but some, whole shiploads of them, didn't even get out of the Gulf of Mexico because the German U-Boats were waiting in the shipping lanes to attack supply and troop ships. Her voice quivered and she went off into the living room to be by herself for a few minutes.

From that day on, I believe Mammaw never picked up a hitchhiking soldier without thinking of the ones she would never be able to pick up. She thought of Uncle Jack, his brother Oslin, and her nephew George E. Lusk fighting somewhere in Europe. Whenever she picked up an airman, she thought of Uncle Jack's brother A. Y. fling a Lockheed Lightning over

227

Germany. Whenever she picked up a sailor, she thought of her younger nephew Charles Patton, her "little Pat," on a ship somewhere in the Pacific. And she always had a brief painful moment thinking of Arnold Patterson from Oklahoma whom she had known and given rides to for such a short, short time.

And sometimes she would gasp and sit up straight in the car and look to the side of the road when it began to drizzle. She wouldn't stop, but she would raise her left hand and touch the back of her fingers to her forehead and then to the window glass. Her eyes would glisten with tears as she drove on further up the road where perhaps there were other young men waiting for rides.

With a heavy heart and a sense of purpose, she continued to "do her part."

Brit Bailey's Prairie

by Joy Nord

Angleton, Texas

Texas ghost lore would not be complete without the staple of fiction entwined among the facts. The legend of Brit Bailey is no exception. To better understand the mystery light located along State Highway 35, in Brazoria County, one must be enlightened to this Texan's courage, integrity, and eccentric behavior.

James Briton Bailey, born in North Carolina on August 1, 1779, was a descendant of Kenneth Bailey whose ancestor, Robert Bruce, once reigned as the King of Scotland. At a young age, "Brit" married Edith Smith and the couple had six children. After Edith's death in 1815, Brit married her sister, Dorothy (also called Nancy), and they had five children, four of them born in Texas. Even as a young man, Brit Bailey had a wandering spirit. He moved frequently, living in Kentucky and Tennessee. During the War of 1812, he served as a U.S. Navy Captain. While residing in Kentucky, Bailey served in the state legislature. However his controversial disposition and an unfavorable reputation caused trouble amid his colleagues. Convicted of forgery and he paid his debt to society in the Kentucky State Penitentiary.

After being released in 1818 Bailey, his family, and six adult slaves sailed from New Orleans to Anahuac, Texas. He settled near the Brazos River on land he allegedly purchased from the Spanish government that gave him recognition as one of the first Anglo settlers in Texas. He built a cabin on Bennett's Ridge, the highest point on his land.

In 1821, after Mexico acquired independence from Spain, the Mexican government disputed his land title. Two years later, Stephan F. Austin received permission from the Mexican Congress to bring three hundred Anglo families to Texas. During this time Bailey's questionable land claim fell under Austin's jurisdiction, and therefore Austin assigned Bailey's land to Martin Varner. A letter addressed to Bailey on October 3, 1823 stated: "You are hereby notified that you cannot be received as a settler in this colony and that you will not be permitted to live nearer the Brazos River than the San Jacinto River nor nearer the Colorado River than the Guadalupe River. You have sixty days to remove your family and property."

Meanwhile, Austin reported to Governor Garcia that he was forced to vacate Bailey and four others from the colony because as Austin said, "These men are of infamous character and have bad conduct. All of them are fugitives from the United States, one for having committed murder, and the others for having counterfeited money."

When Austin showed up at Bailey's cabin to enforce the eviction order, he was greeted by Brit's shotgun barrel. Austin confronted Bailey about serving time in the Kentucky prison for forgery. Bailey did not deny the allegation but told Austin it wasn't the time he spent in the state pen that caused his embarrassment, but the term he served in the Kentucky legislature that bothered his conscience. On July 7, 1824, noted as one of the "Old Three Hundred," Austin decided to honor Bailey's original claim of a league of land on the east bank of the Brazos River, known as Bailey's Prairie.

Although Austin never liked Bailey, he assembled settlers from the lower Brazos River region to Bailey's home where they took the oath to defend the Mexican Constitution of 1824. During this same meeting, at Austin's request, Bailey became a lieutenant in the newly formed militia company. In September, he took part in the Battle of Jones Creek along with twenty-three other men to fight cannibalistic Karankawa Indians. One of Brit's sons, Phelps, died in this battle. In 1832 Bailey fought in the Battle of Velasco, the first bloodshed between Texas and Mexico; Bailey's sons, Smith and Gaines, were among the twenty-seven Texans wounded. Later, Smith died at the Alamo. Brit's youngest living son, James, drowned in a Brazos River flood within a few years after the family arrived. None of the sons born in Texas lived past their first year or so.

Brit Bailey became a successful cattle rancher and cotton grower. Gradually he expanded his land holdings from Houston south to the Gulf Coast. Although Bailey could portray a respectable citizen, he gained the reputation of being an instigator, and was a constant thorn in Austin's side, mainly because of by his love for liquor and a good fight. Brit often took the law into his own hands, ruling the area with a cracking bullwhip and a loaded shotgun. His practical jokes and his pursuit of a fight, to anyone, anytime, and anywhere, managed to infuriate a number of early settlers. Reportedly, he would shoot a cigar from a man's mouth, and say, "I don't miss very often." When bored, or a little too intoxicated, he would pick a fight just for spite. His drinking escapades usually led to embarrassment, not his but that of the poor soul he was bullying. On more than one occasion, Brit fired shots at a man's feet to watch him dance a jig. One night he set fire to his own corncrib and then sat back under an old oak tree with his whiskey jug to admire the flames. He probably would have set fire to the house too if his favorite daughter hadn't convinced him otherwise. Possibly some folks were glad when "Old Brit" finally died, for those who knew him probably thought he died from meanness. But history claims that he surrendered to cholera on December 6, 1832.

Brit Bailey had some unusual request about his burial stated in his will, which still exists. He demanded to be buried standing because he had never stooped to any man while alive, and didn't intend to after his death. He wanted to be buried facing the west because all of his life he had moved toward the west and that's the direction he wanted to be in when he crossed over to the other side. He also wanted his rifle placed over his shoulder with his powder horn by his side, and a full jug of whiskey planted at his feet. Buried in the family graveyard, not far from his red house, all of Bailey's instructions were followed except one – the jug of whiskey.

Several stories as to why the jug never made it into Old Brit's coffin have materialized over the years. One account suggests the slaves that dug the grave stole it. If this is true, and Old Brit was really as mean as folks claimed, his slaves probably did confiscate the whiskey and returned with it later that night to celebrate and dance a little jig on top of their master's grave. Another tale claims that his wife refused to allow the "devil's brew" into the coffin. When a favorite servant brought the whiskey jug into the house to place at Bailey's feet, Mrs. Bailey refused. Supposedly, she grabbed the jug and threw it out the window. She thought her husband had drunk plenty of the stuff here on earth and he could do without it in the after life. No matter which story is the truth, Brit's whiskey jug never made it into his grave, which explains his restless afterlife. Old Brit's ghost wanders the area as a white orb, known as "Bailey's light" in search of more whiskey.

Apparently Brit Bailey began to haunt his wife shortly after his death. Within four years Mrs. Bailey sold the house and land to Mr. and Mrs. Thomas. Not long afterwards, the Thomas family realized that Old Brit had failed to cross over to the other side.

On one moonless night Mrs. Thomas, forced to sleep alone while her husband was away on business was suddenly awakened by a strange presence in the bedroom. She gazed around the room and saw strange form that shadowed the doorway. Too frightened to scream out, she watched the figure drift toward her. When it reached the foot of her bed it stooped as if looking for something under the bed, and then returned to the doorway and disappeared. Malinda, the servant girl, who had also been awakened by the presence, informed her mistress that Brit Bailey had died in that bedroom where Mrs. Thomas had been sleeping!

When John Thomas returned from his trip, Ann told him of her experience, and that she would never sleep in that room again. She had already switched bedrooms. Although he had heard rumors that the place was haunted before he purchased it, he accused his wife of having an overactive imagination and agreed to sleep in the room just to prove there was nothing to fear. A few nights later, Mrs. Thomas, asleep across the hall, awoke to an alarming scream. When she entered the other bedroom she found her husband sitting on the side of the bed drenched in sweat and shaken with fear. Not long afterwards, John and Ann Thomas moved.

Beginning in the 1850s Bailey's ghost took on a light form. One night Colonel Mordello Munson, who had a plantation home on the edge of Bailey's Prairie, saw a column of light about the size of a man. Although it was some distance away, he and a friend chased it all night but were never able to get close to the mysterious light. In 1939, Robert and Joe Munson observed a floating light about basketball size within the trees of the prairie. In 1946, Robert Munson saw it again in the same location as before. In December 1953, a couple sighted the ghost light along the highway. And in 1960, a woman claimed to have seen the light, but became too distraught to share her experience.

Throughout the years, Bailey's light has decreased in size and strength. Some people around Brazoria County claim the ghostly orb presents itself every seventh year. No matter when the well-known phenomenon light appears, whether by day or night, it disappears just as quickly. Old Brit has yet to find his jug of whiskey, and probably never will.

In 1970 to commemorate Brit Bailey's life, the Texas Historical Commission placed two markers near Bailey's Prairie: Angleton (Brazoria County) State Highway 35, 5 miles NE at his grave, Munson Plantation, and East Columbia (Brazoria County) SH 35, 2 miles E in roadside park.

Bear Creek Bridge
on Patterson Road
by Marybeth G.

Houston, Texas

Tap. Tap. Tap. The car full of curious teenagers parked on Bear Creek Bridge at Patterson Road between State Highway 6 and Eldridge Road in Houston, heard tapping all over the car, faint but distinct. Not the sound of the car settling. Not the sound of something blown by the wind; there was no wind that hot, sultry summer night. Nothing that could be explained by anything they could see. They shone their flashlights and a high-powered spotlight through the car windows in every direction. Nothing was there. But the tapping continued.

Shaken a bit, the teens drove away but hadn't gone far when the driver, frustrated that he'd given in to fear, turned the car around and headed back. Just before they got back to the bridge he pulled over and told his girlfriend to take the wheel. After protesting for a minute or two, she did as he said, driving slowly onto the bridge and stopping again. He opened the door and jumped out.

"Now leave me!" he demanded.

She stared at him in horror. "You're crazy!"

"Go!" he repeated. "Leave me here. I want to try something and see what happens. I'll be fine. I'll call you on my cell phone if I need you. Get out of here – now!"

She left hesitantly, driving slowly and looking over her shoulder every few seconds until she could no longer see his silhouette outlined against the dim reflection of Houston's city lights that made it through the canopy of trees covering the road.

She decided to loop around the road and come back the opposite way. Barely two minutes later, her cell phone rang.

"Come back now!" her boyfriend screamed, "Hurry!" Seconds later they were back on the bridge. He just stood there.

"What's wrong?" she asked, reaching out to him and then recoiling in fright. The other teens pulled him into the car before she pressed the gas and took off, tires screeching in the sodden blackness. He was cold, so cold that he chilled the air between them and the skin on his arm where she touched him felt like one of those rubber gloves in a Halloween House of Horrors.

"Go! Just go!" he screamed, huddling over and rocking back and forth.

She sped away, slowing down only when she reached a well-lit convenience store parking lot, where she pulled in and parked beneath a security light.

When she turned to her boyfriend, the security light caught glistening trails on his face where tears streamed down his cheeks. He was still shaking and very cold even though it was a hot summer night with temperatures in the eighties. Gradually he stopped shaking and was able to talk about what happened. He said he had not been able to move at all when they dropped him off. It was as if something had been preventing him from moving away from the bridge. He'd had overwhelming feelings of sadness and anger. As soon as the car drove away, a violent gust of wind came out of nowhere, with the wind swirling around him. The air kept getting colder and colder. That was when he had panicked and called for help. Now, sweating in the sticky summer air underneath the convenience store security lights, he regained his courage and decided he wanted to go back and try again. He felt there had to be more than one spirit back there, with all the sensations he'd experienced.

Of course, everyone tried to convince him to stay away, or at least to wait until another night. But he would have none of it. He had to go back right then. Anything else would mean that he could be considered a coward.

So they went back.

This time his girlfriend gave him her mobile phone to use as a recorder. Again they drove off slowly and kept looking back. They were barely out of sight when he called this time, screaming loudly, "Get me now!" He ran toward them opened the door before the car came to a complete stop, and dove in beside her, trembling. Again, he was crying and shaking and very, very cold. He said that this time had been much, much worse than the first.

When they got back to the convenience store parking lot, they listened to what he had recorded on his girlfriend's phone. On the recording, the wind had started blowing so hard that it was easy to hear in the background. He described every sensation he felt as it happened: an overwhelming restlessness, fear, anger, a jumble of emotions. Suddenly there was the sound of a woman, screaming and screaming. He said that the wind was blowing so fiercely that the trees were shaking violently, as if in a hurricane, when the woman was screaming.

After hearing the woman's screams on the recording, they all decided they had to go back to see if they could help her. By this time it was after 3 a.m. They stopped the car on Bear Creek Bridge and all got out with their flashlights and searchlight. Holding hands for safety, they looked everywhere but could find nothing amiss. In fact, the bridge now seemed to have become a refuge of peace and quiet. Only croaking frogs and the soft sounds of nocturnal wild animals broke the silence. Even the dark shadows cast by the trees over Patterson Road seemed to have become lighter.

The bridge over Bear Creek on Patterson Road in Houston is near the site of a fierce, bloody battle in the War Between the States. Patterson Road runs between State Highway 6 and Eldridge Road, winding through marshy land and woods, along the edge of Bear Creek Park. Most of the road is overgrown, with dense foliage hanging over the road and blocking off sunlight, creating a dark, tunnel effect even at mid-day.

A couple of hundred years ago this area had been a thriving pioneer farming community of German immigrants and their descendants, with a church and shops in the center of town. The Civil War battle site is in the southeast quadrant of what is now Bear Creek Park. An old, hard-to-find "blue light" cemetery is all that remains of the church and its grounds. The area floods easily and early settlements are said to have been devastated by hurricanes.

Between midnight and 3:00 a.m. it's not uncommon to experience tapping noises and to sense spirits on Bear Creek Bridge. Sometimes, perhaps in an effort to keep nosy strangers away, locals tell visitors to go to another bridge, Langham Creek Bridge, where nothing unusual is likely to happen and the strangers soon grow bored and leave. Nevertheless, many local residents and some visitors are drawn to Bear Creek Bridge where they take photographs of ghostly orbs hovering in mid-air. People also experience chills and unsettling feelings, and watch as compass needles swing wildly without regard for true North. Cell phones also often behave oddly on this stretch of roadway, beeping and flashing erratically. Perhaps most ominously, there have been an exceptionally high number of vehicle accidents on Patterson Road near and on Bear Creek Bridge – some almost all fatal. Oddly enough, the accidents are invariably head-on collisions even though drivers have a half-mile clear visibility.

Overpass of the Dead

by Marybeth Gradziel

Humble, Texas

A few years back, there used to be repeated anonymous warning nailed to telephone poles along Farm to Market Road 1960 in Humble, just northeast of Houston: *IF YOU ATTEMPT TO GO TO THIS AREA PLEASE USE EXTREME CAUTION. THERE HAVE BEEN MURDERS AND BODIES UNCOVERED IN THE WOODS.*

As John tells it now, when he saw the abandoned church back then, with its doors chained shut and guarded by a huge white crossarms stretched out against the forces of evil, he was almost overcome by an anxiety attack. Not like him to get spooked like that. Not like him at all, then or now. But as he took the old downtown Humble exit, off of Farm to Market Road 1960 and u-turned underneath the off ramp along the railroad tracks, he started to have chest pains – lightly at first, then growing stronger as he looked around at the other closed buildings. John saw what had been a movie theater, the remains of a miniature golf course by the abandoned church and a warehouse. All were closed up, bolted and chained shut. There was no one else around but he still felt as if he were being watched. Dark forest had grown up to the roadside. Straggly branches reached out and scratched against the remains of shattered window. He heard screeching like fingernails on chalkboard although there was no wind, not even a breeze. The stench was more than swampy. It burned the inside of his nostrils and made him want to puke.

As the chest pains subsided, John's breathing returned to normal, however, every hair on his body was straight up. Undaunted, he pulled out his digital camera, batteries freshly charged hours earlier, and hit "on." It flickered briefly and turned itself off. He tried again and got the dead battery indicator, so he switched to his backup battery set – also just recharged – but the camera turned off again and whenever he tried, he got a dead battery icon.

The pains started coming back, and gasping for air, he jumped back in his car and hightailed it out of there. He'd come back, he vowed. He wasn't a sissy. He'd be back, but not alone. Next time he'd bring friends.

When he got home he checked the camera again, just for grins. It worked perfectly.

He popped the batteries in the battery charger and pressed the test switch. They were all fully charged.

The East Farm to Market Road 1960 Overpass was built over land that had been a cemetery by, and likely predating, the railroad tracks. Some said there had been head stones dating back to the Confederacy. Gravestones, which were moved, and presumably made it through the move more or less intact, and which still can be read date back as far as 1898. When the Overpass was built, the old graveyard beneath the overpass ramp was dug up and the contents of the grave moved deeper into the woods, mixed with the graves at what is now known as the Humble Negro Cemetery.

The re-established cemetery holds veterans from both World War I and World War II and a child's grave, from the early 1900s. "Some of the tombs have been broken open by cattle that marched through the dense woods over the years. Other gravestones are scattered or knocked over. Many names or dates are unreadable," says Charles Cunningham, head of a volunteer group working to restore the cemetery at the re-established site and have it designated a Historical Burial Site.

Charles Bender, owner of the Bender Sawmill, gave the land to the African-American citizens who worked his sawmill so they would have a place to bury their dead. The cemetery is extremely secluded. There is no road and it can only be reached by hiking through the thorny underbrush. Ancient pine trees tower over the graves, shading them from the burning Texas sun. Wild vines twine everywhere, tripping the unwary hiker.

The Overpass and land around it – the original cemetery - especially the dark, dank woods with pockets of oozing muck, have gained a reputation as an area ruled by Evil spirits. Reportedly there have been demonic voices calling forth from the now abandoned buildings, even with the doors closed and locked firmly. There is a bench just outside the former Putt Putt golf course where a white, human-like figure sits on the far side every night. When the Old Dollar Theater was open, workers were attacked by an entity or entities that would throw things at them and corner them with dark shadows. A Holy Water Blessing was done and a cross was posted in the main projection booth, but every day the cross turned up, inexplicably, in another booth. When the theater opened for the day, there would sometimes be voices from the projection rooms or the sound of footsteps in the hall but there would be no one there. One morning the projectionist found the word "Satan" carved into the wall of the main projection booth, the location of most of the noises and violent attacks.

Spectral figures and red lights have been seen in the gloomy woods encroaching upon the railroad tracks. One local resident calls the woods "Pure Evil" and some neighbors consider the area to be a gateway to Hell. Some say that almost all the ghosts seen here appear as rotting corpses, giving credence to those who explain that this area is haunted because the cemetery was desecrated when it was moved. In any case, the area is certainly creepy and has a powerfully unsettling effect on locals and visitors alike.

Today, the path to the railroads tracks and the woods creeping up to them is blocked by a high chain link fence with barbed wire strung on top – a strong physical deterrent erected recently by someone, possibly to save lives. Underneath the gloomy overpass, everything is shadowy and cold. The sounds of traffic overhead reverberate eerily, reminiscent of demonic whispers.

The Myth of Sarah Jane Road
by Janelle Fears

Port Neches, Texas

"Sarah Jane, Sarah Jane, where are you my Sarah Jane?"

Sarah Jane Road in Port Neches is the site of a familiar ghost story for area residents. The story continues to have a life of its own, regardless of denials by the Block family. A large tract of property surrounding the road and bridge in question was owned by the Block family before this property was later bought in the 1940s by Jefferson Chemical Company (later renamed the Huntsman Chemical Company). This area is swampy, and has dense thickets of tall, imposing, cypress trees. Thick mists arise from waterways and provide a scary visage that seems to be the origin of old legends about Sarah Jane. The Huntsman Chemical Plant adding to mists through chemical emission into the waterways has been partially blamed for the incessant ghost stories.

The spirit of Sarah Jane is said to be searching the marsh and thicket for her baby whom she supposedly drowned. Another story says that Sarah Jane was hanged from a cypress tree near a broken down old bridge due to this horrible deed. A third version describes Civil War Confederate soldiers chasing Union sympathizer Sarah Jane in her wagon, off the bridge, into the water. Sarah Jane was shot while trying to save her baby in the river, and the infant met an untimely death as well.

Information provided by Sarah Jane's son, W.T. Block, Jr., discredits all myths about his mother's involvement as a "Union sympathizer." In fact Sarah Jane Sweeney was born in 1884 (a full nineteen years after the war) in Grand Chenier, Louisiana and moved to Texas in 1906. She married W.T. Block, one of the founding fathers of Port Neches, in 1919. Sarah Jane died in 1983 at an old age of 99 years. All her children were said to have survived with none being drowned.

This area is different from most in the Gulf Coast bay, and is described to be more like deep East Texas. It is a popular place to take children during Halloween because of misty bogs, thickets, and intense darkness. Some people claim while standing on the bridge they have seen a spirit figure of Sarah Jane, and have heard the sound of crying from Sarah Jane and her baby. While others say if you stand on the bridge at midnight you can see a flickering light in the woods that resembles the glow of an old lantern and you can hear Sarah Jane's moans and hollers. As most legends go, they just get better over time. Nowadays it is said that on Friday the 13th if you stand on the bridge, you can actually see the ghost of Sarah Jane wandering in the woods with her lantern in search of her baby.

The one and only connection to Sarah Jane and her namesake stretch of road was a work of fiction written by a Port Arthur newspaper writer years ago. The Block family set the record straight in a "*Midcounty Chronicle*" article by Carl Cunningham, Jr. in October, 1998.

Local residents have said the following about Sarah Jane Road: "I've never seen anything too spooky out there save for the occasional gang of hungry raccoons"; "The scariest thing I have seen out there at night is a roving alligator looking for a meal."; and "People bring their kids out here on Halloween night to scare them."

Whether there is any truth to the legend or not, whether it involves the named woman or some other restless spirit, I guess that is how the story has been passed through the years – the mysterious tale of Sarah Jane and her infant child.